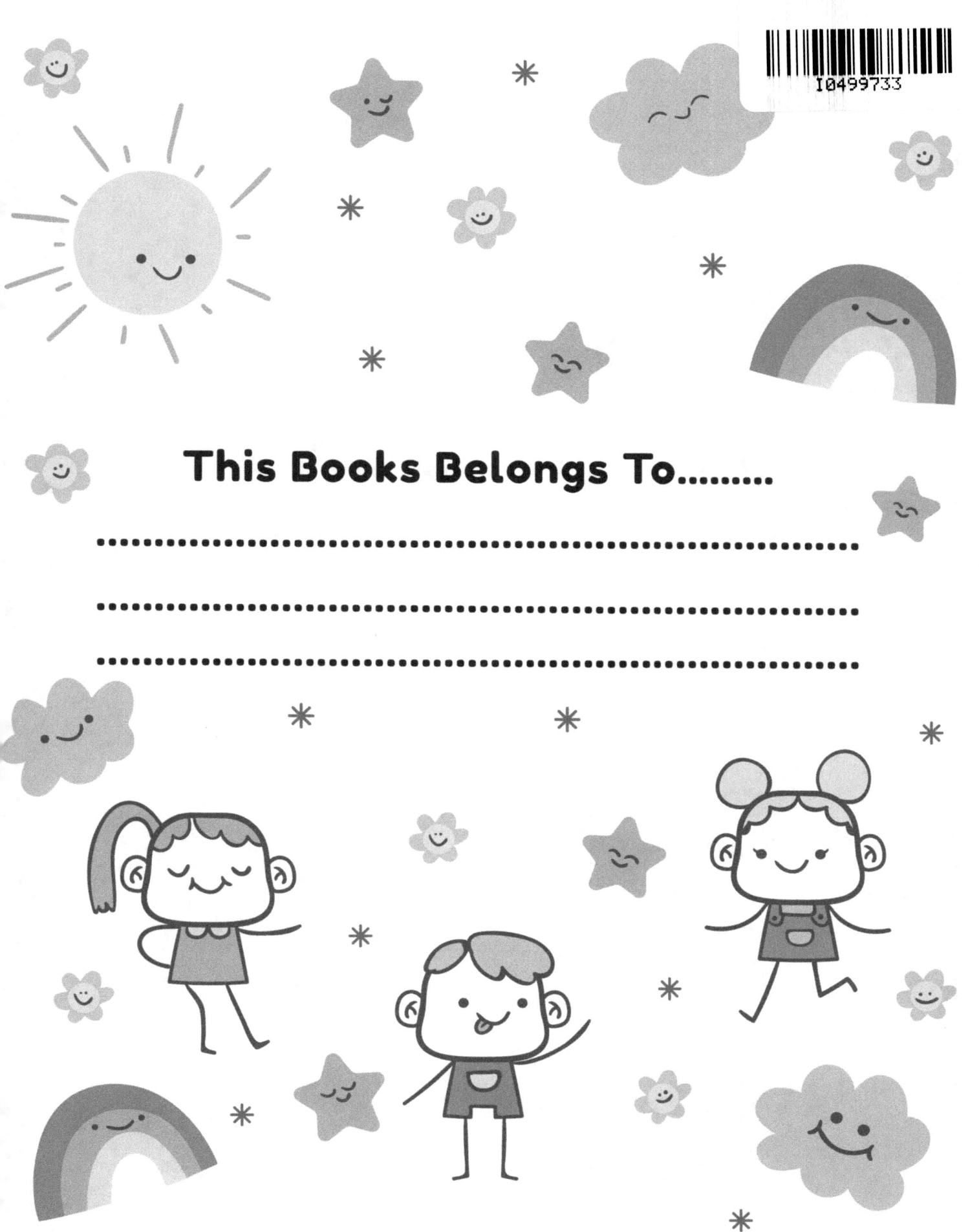

This Books Belongs To.........

....

....

....

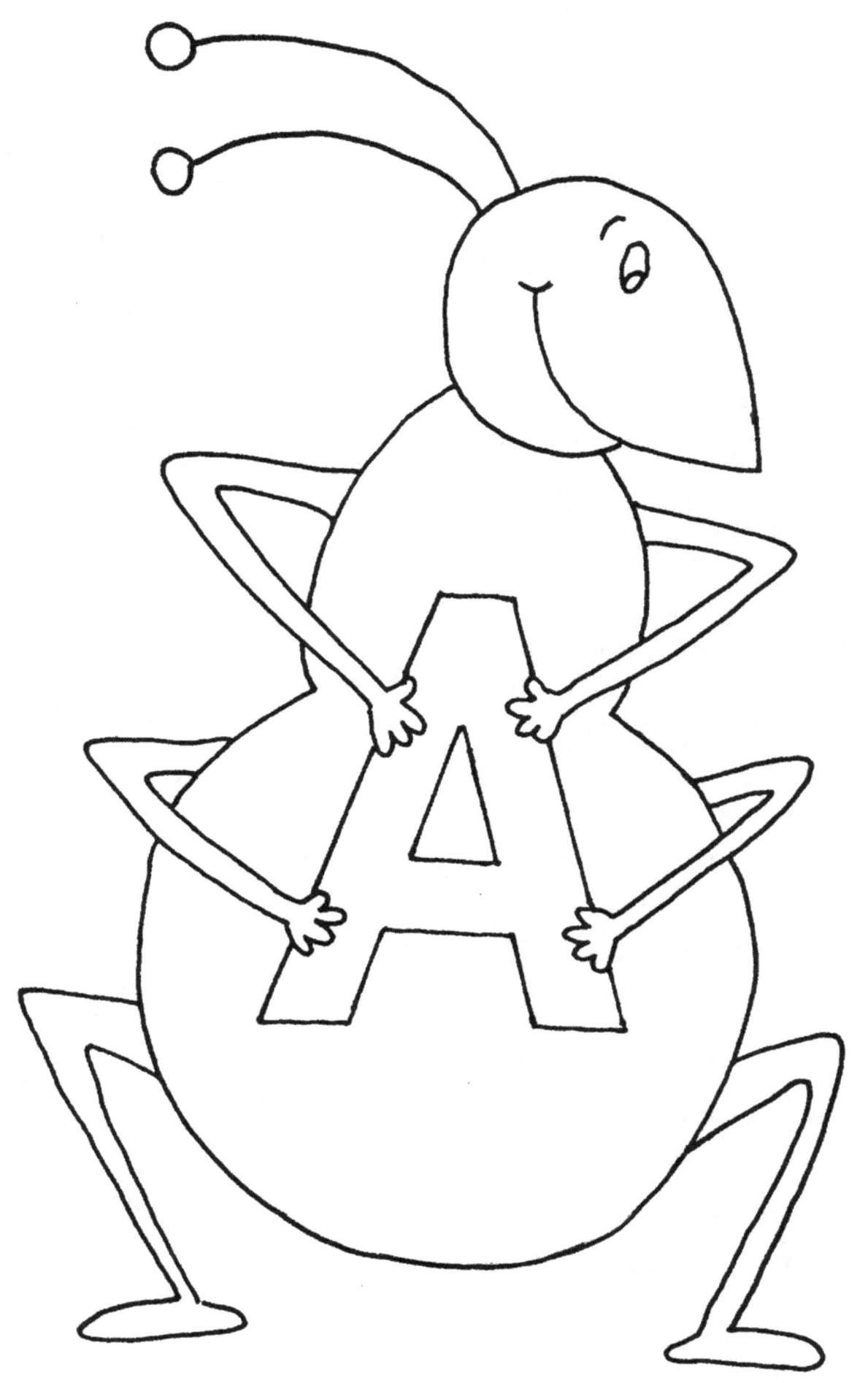

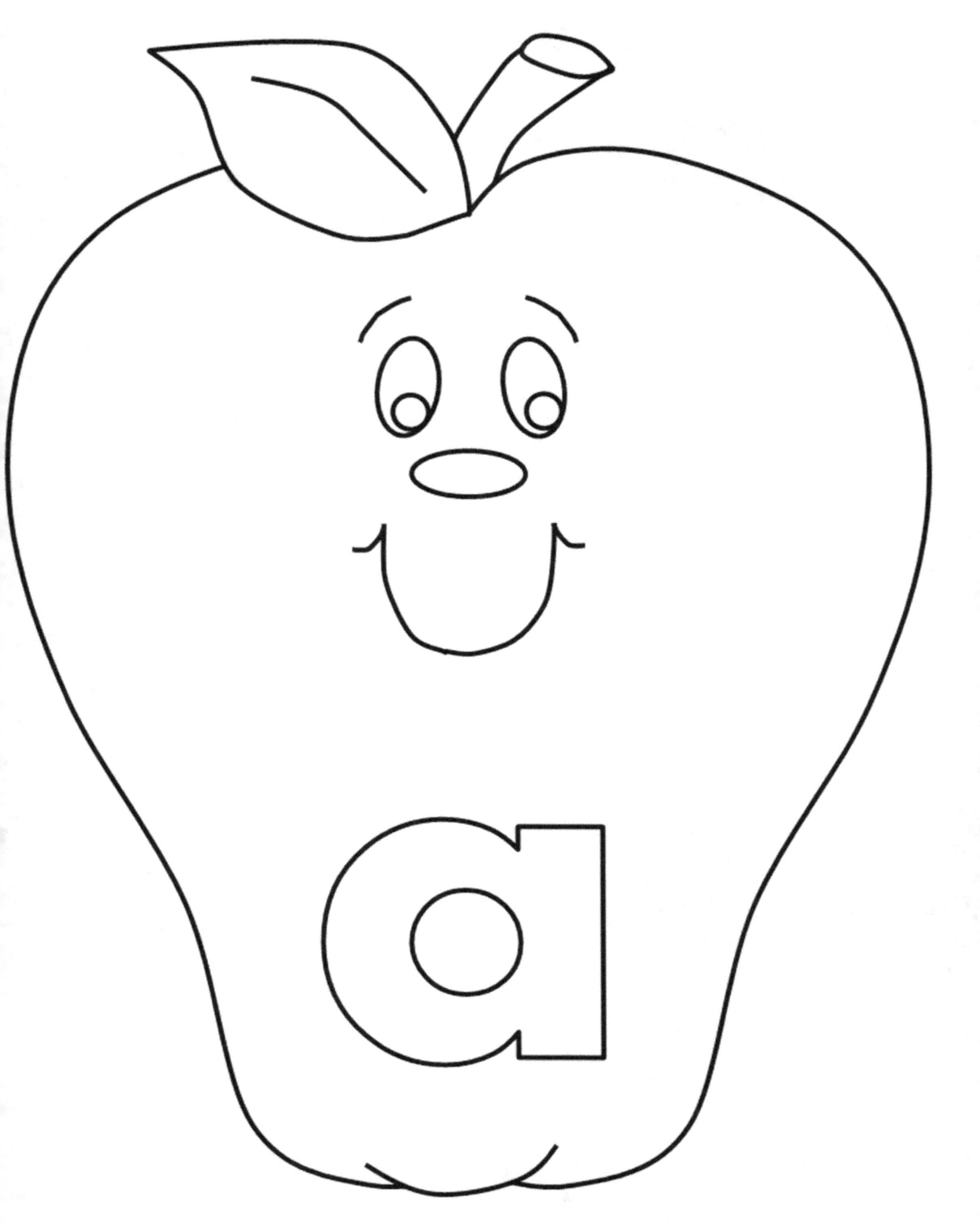

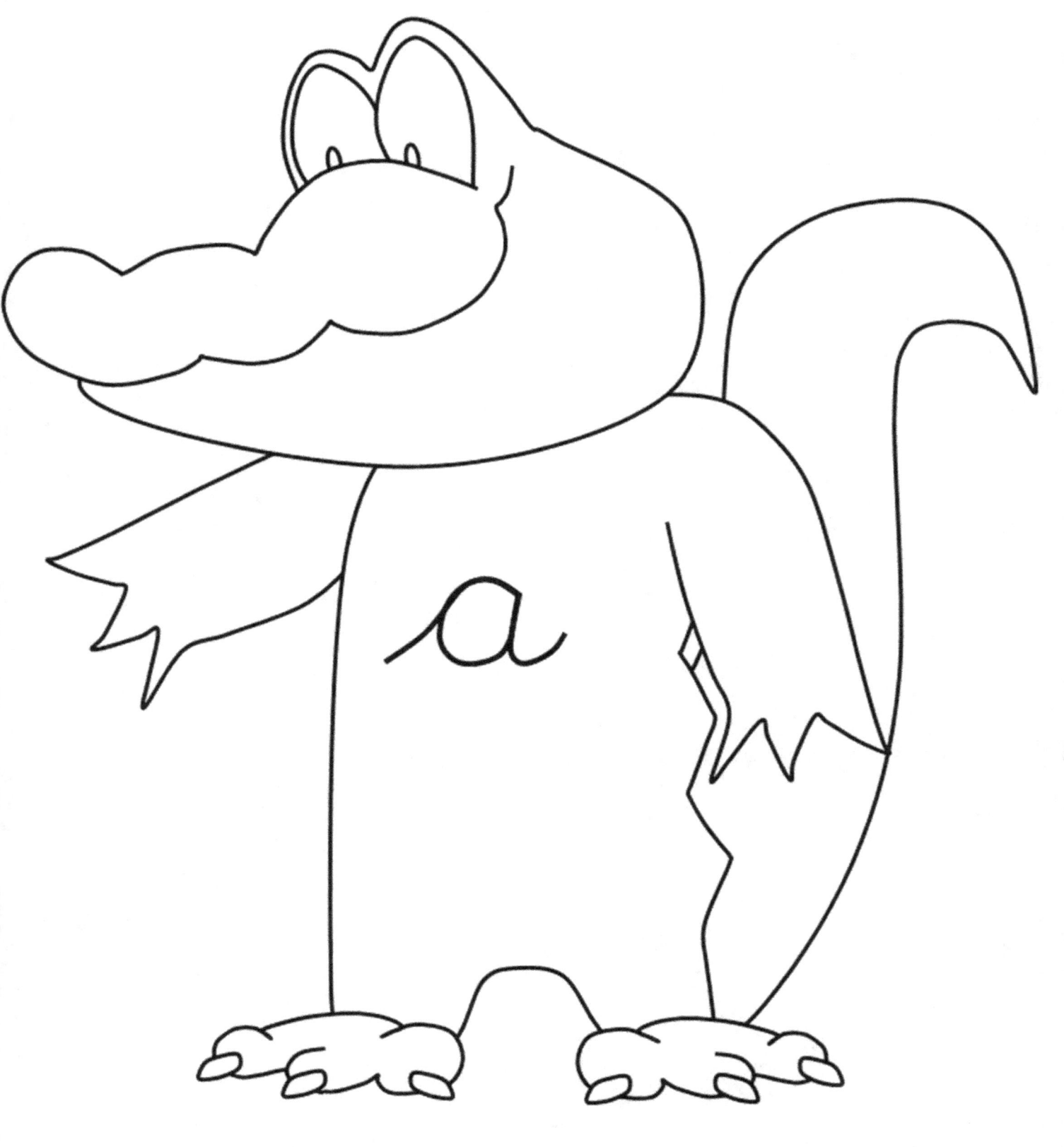

Trace the steps for making the letter a on the following line.

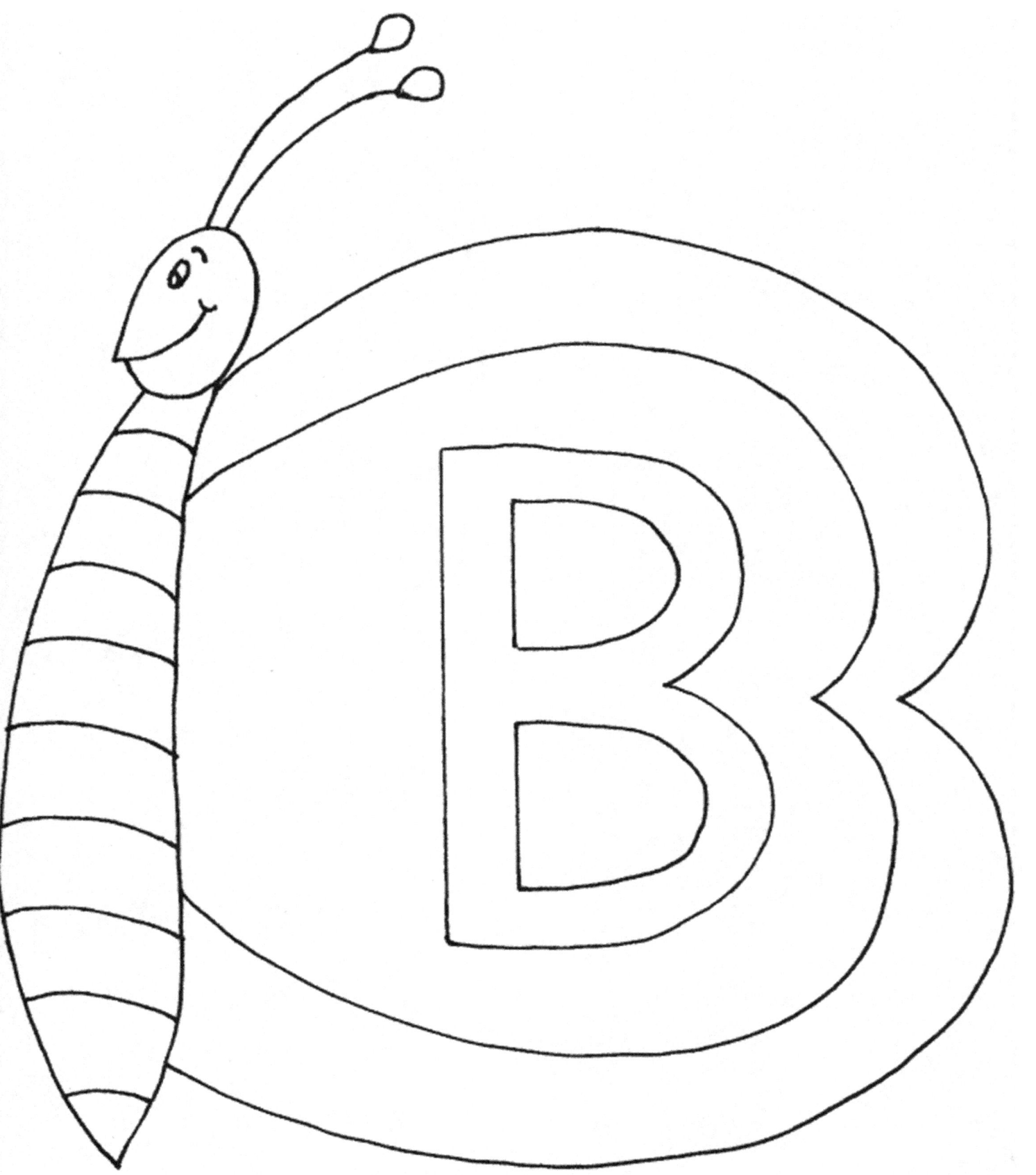

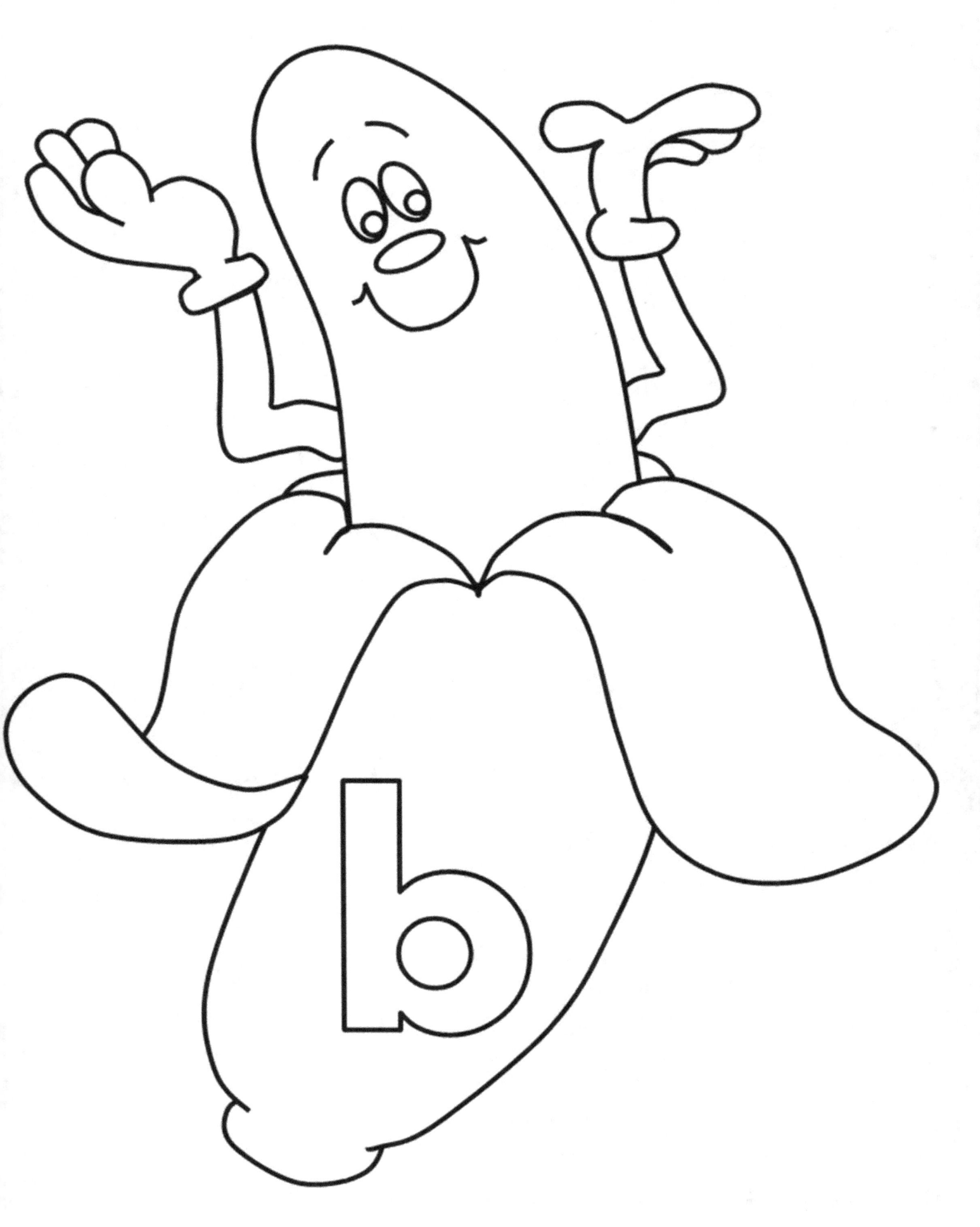

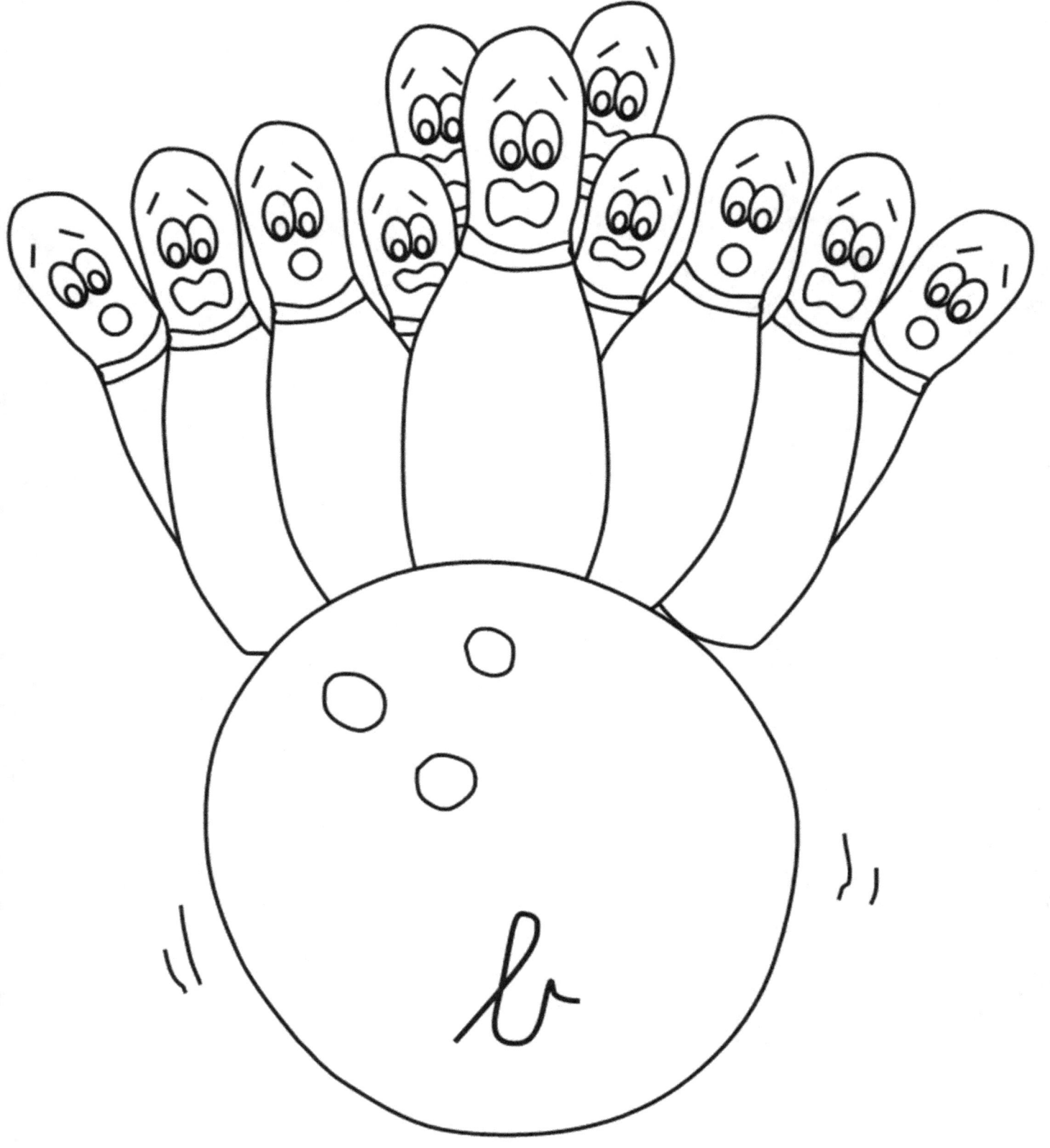

Trace the steps for making the letter b on the following line.

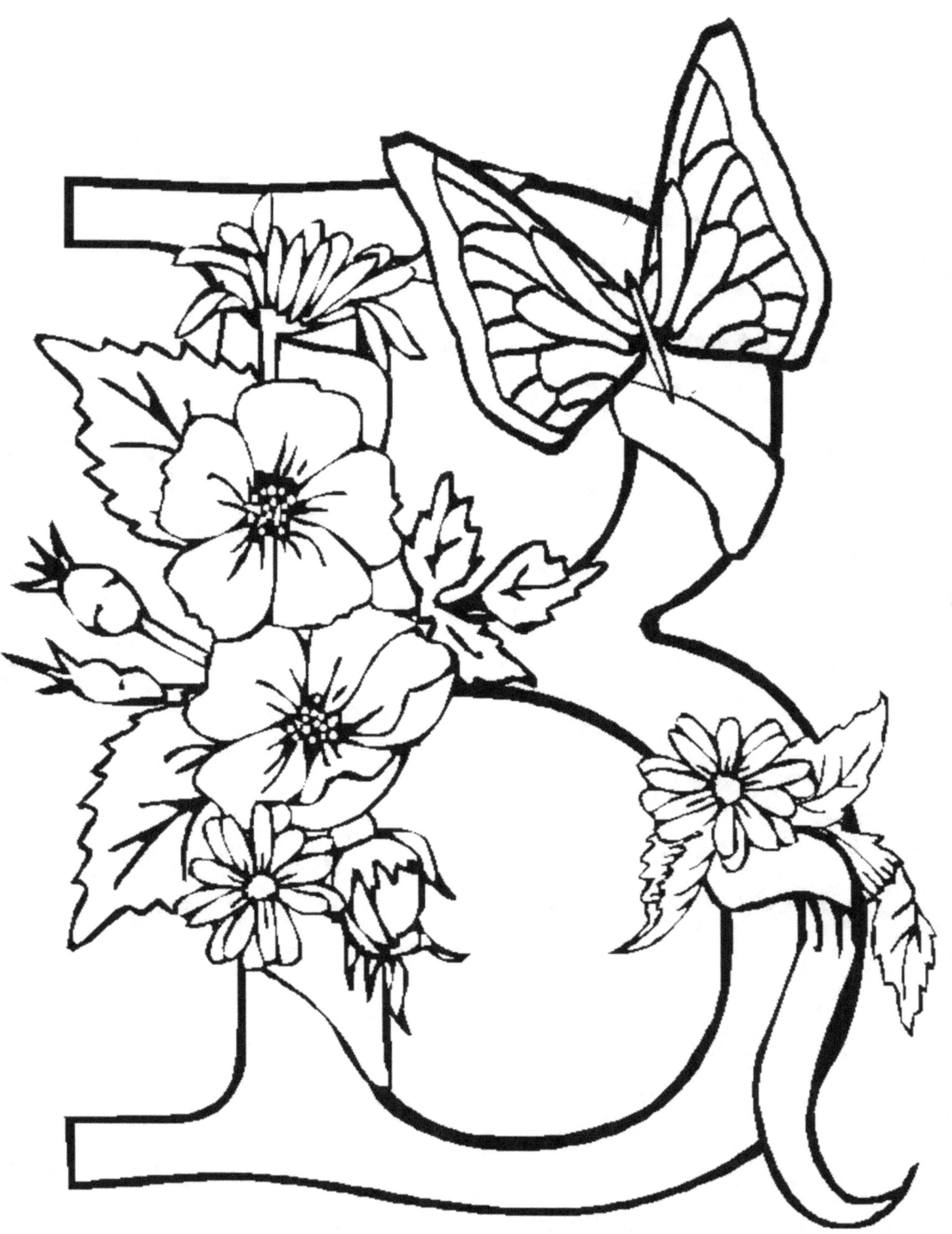

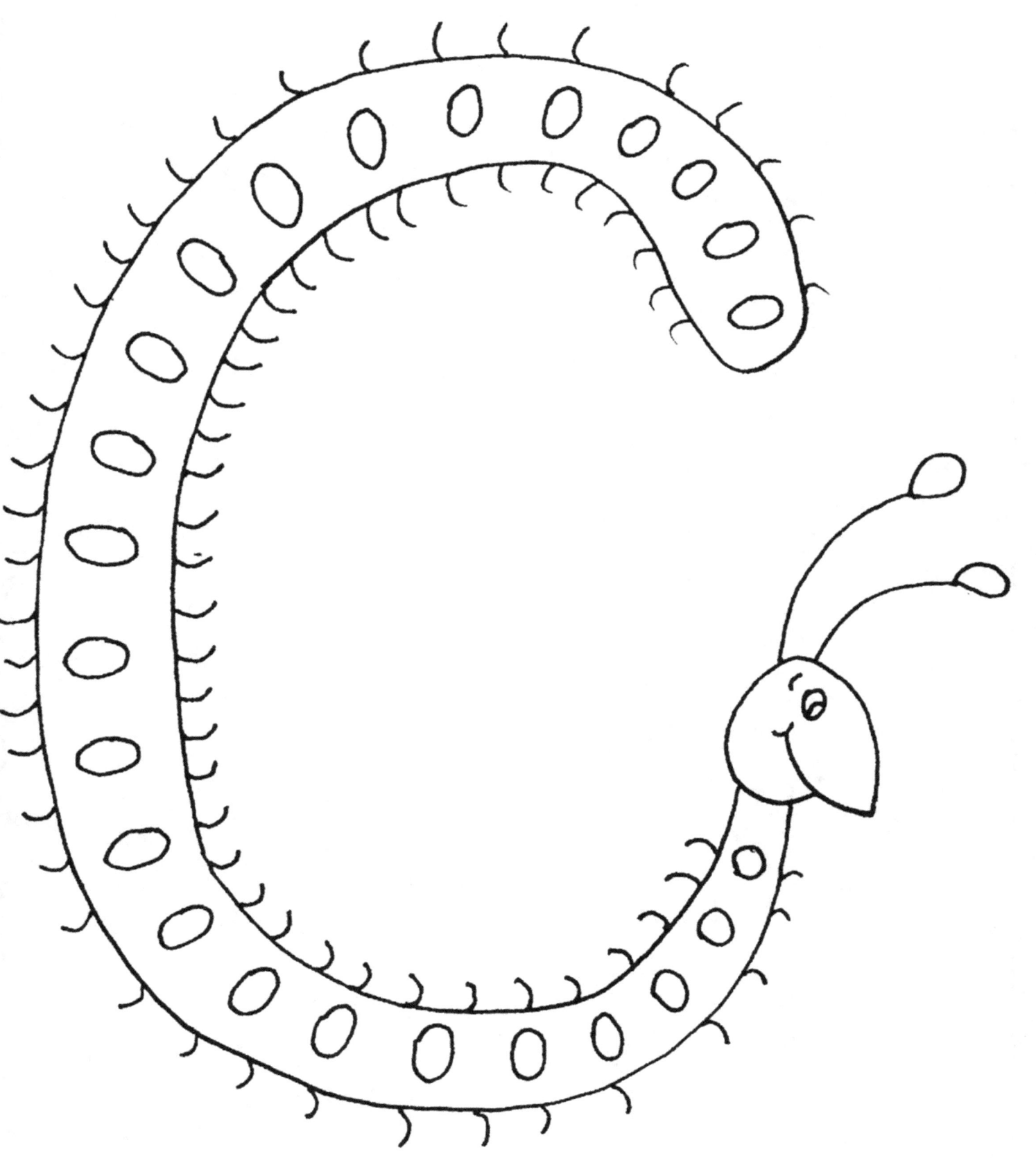

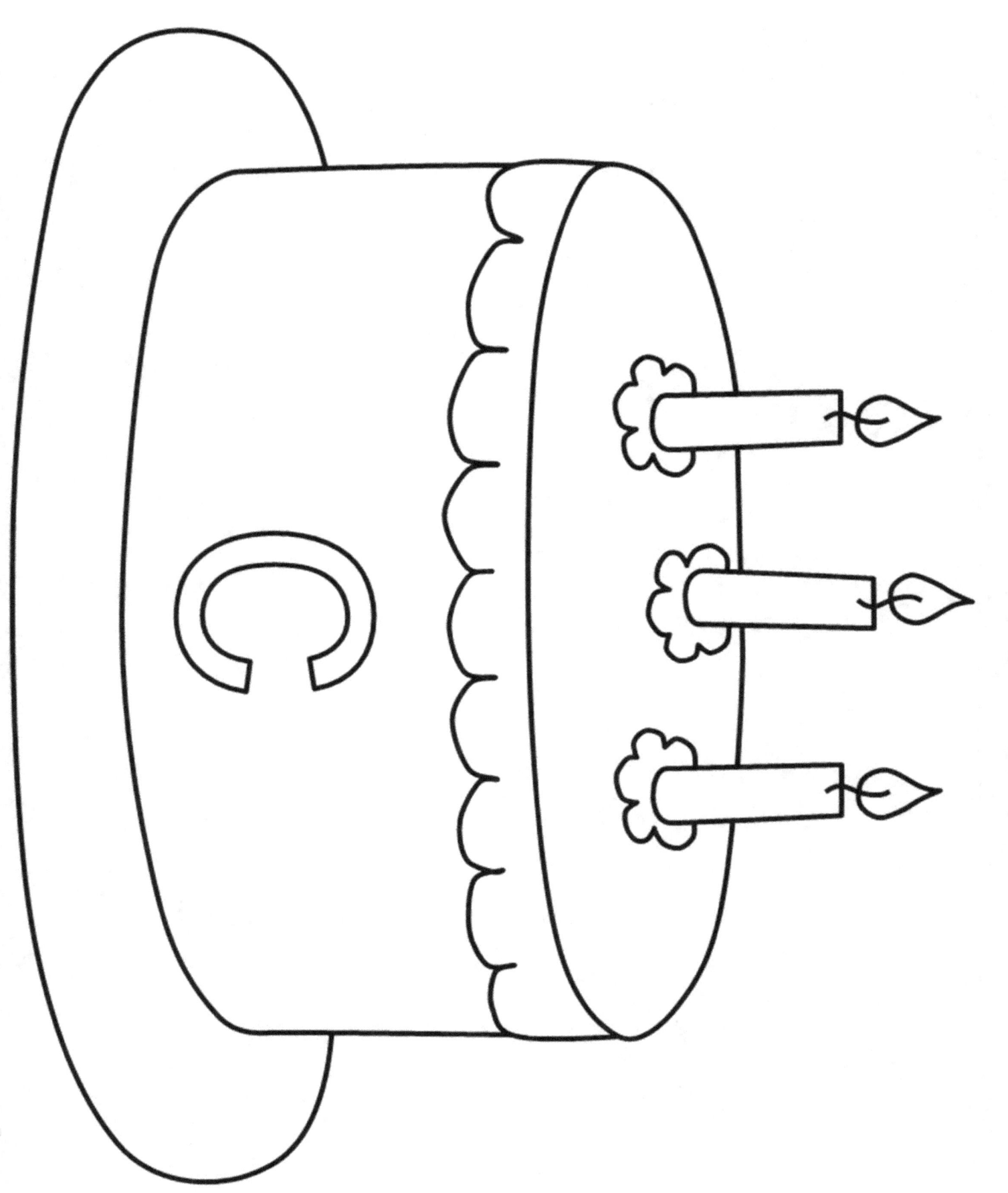

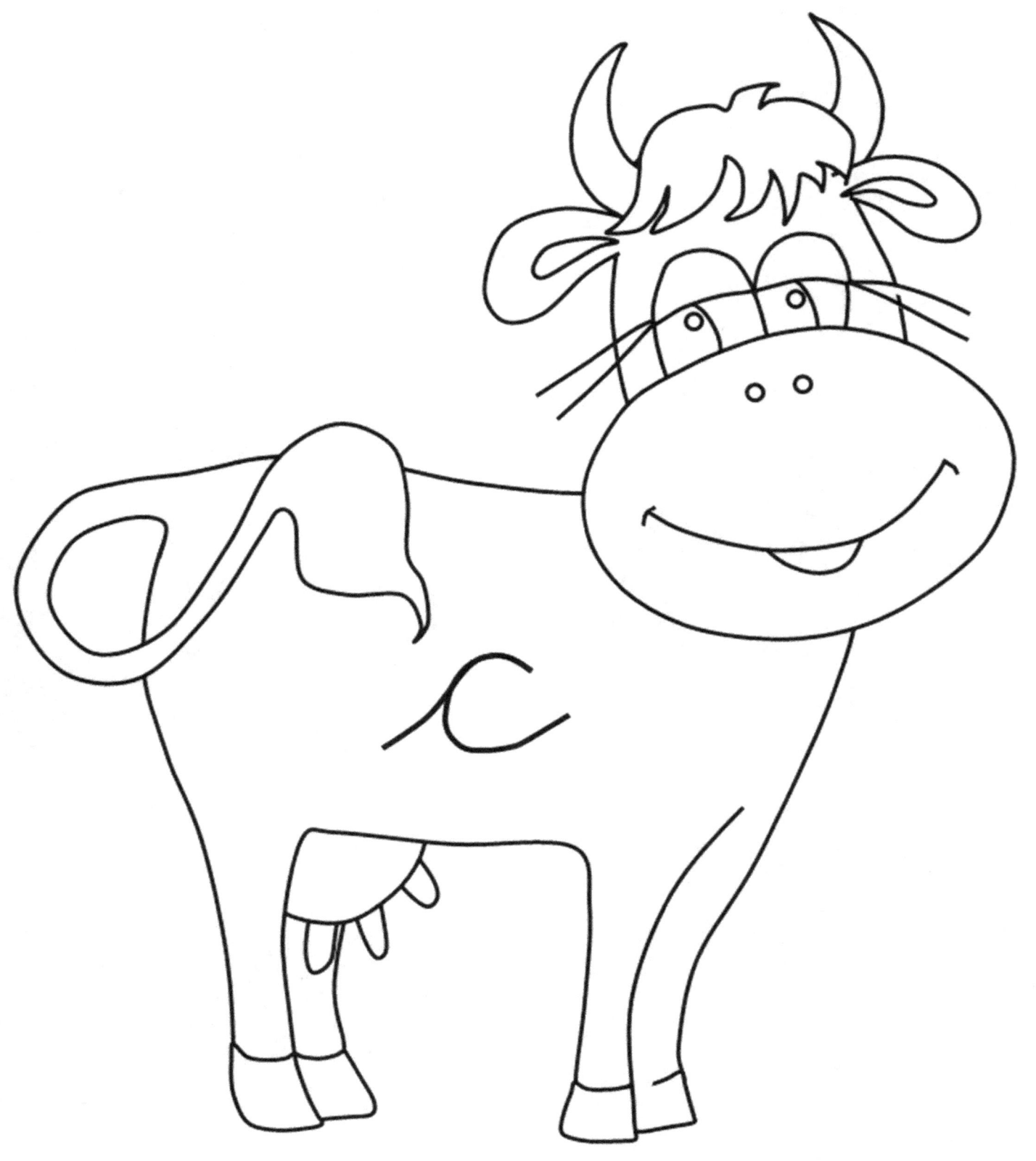

Trace the steps for making the letter c on the following line.

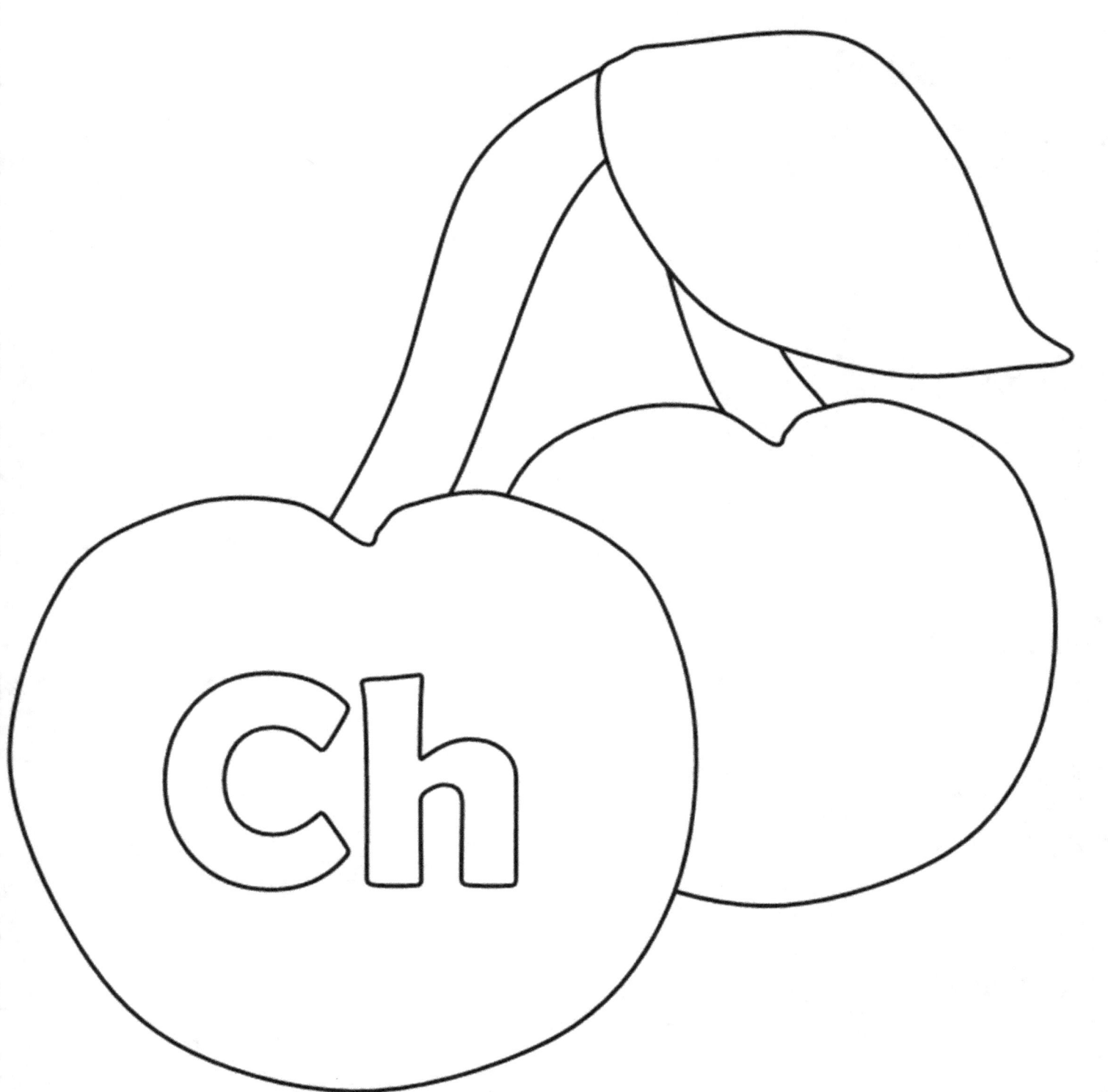

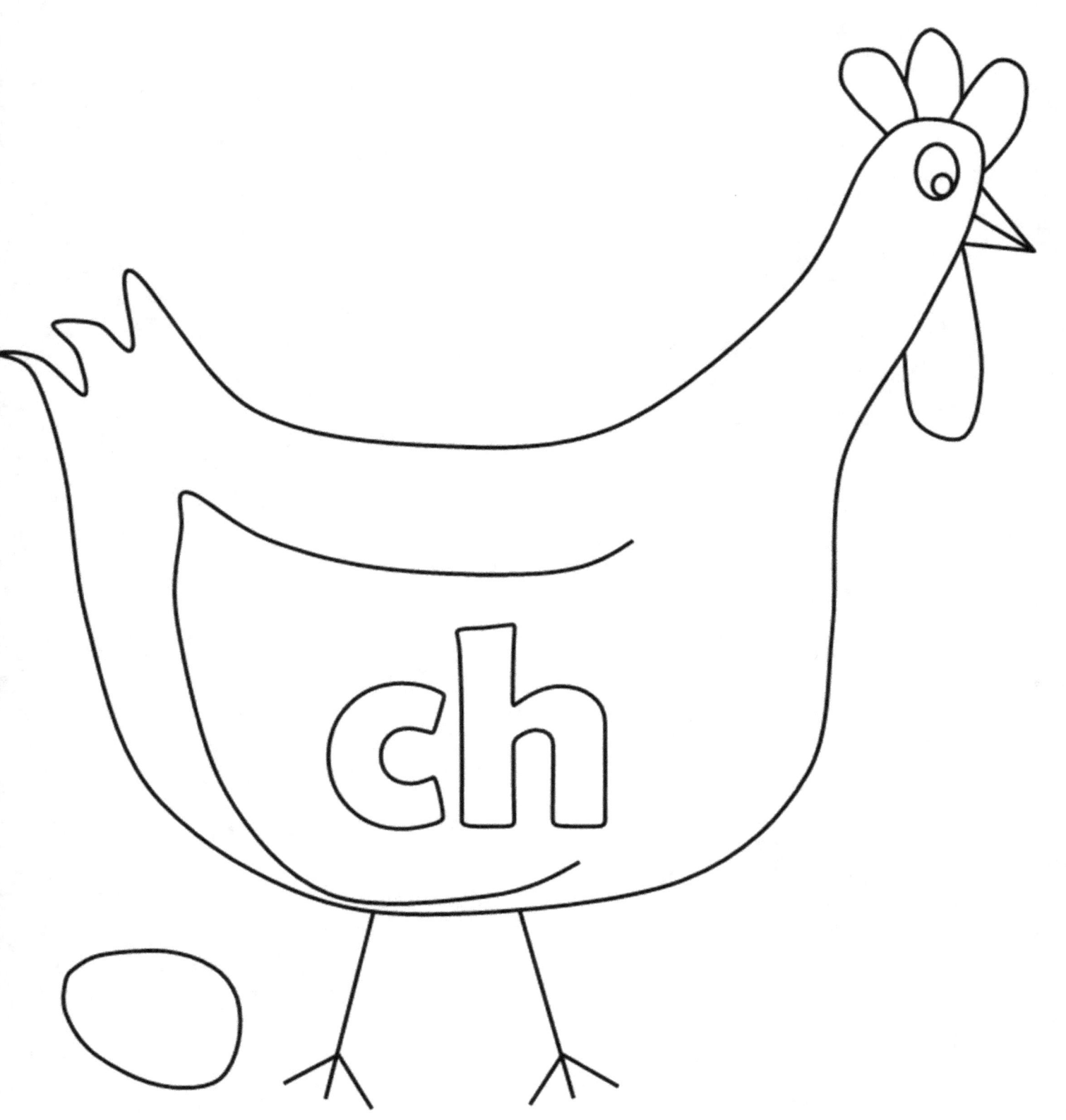

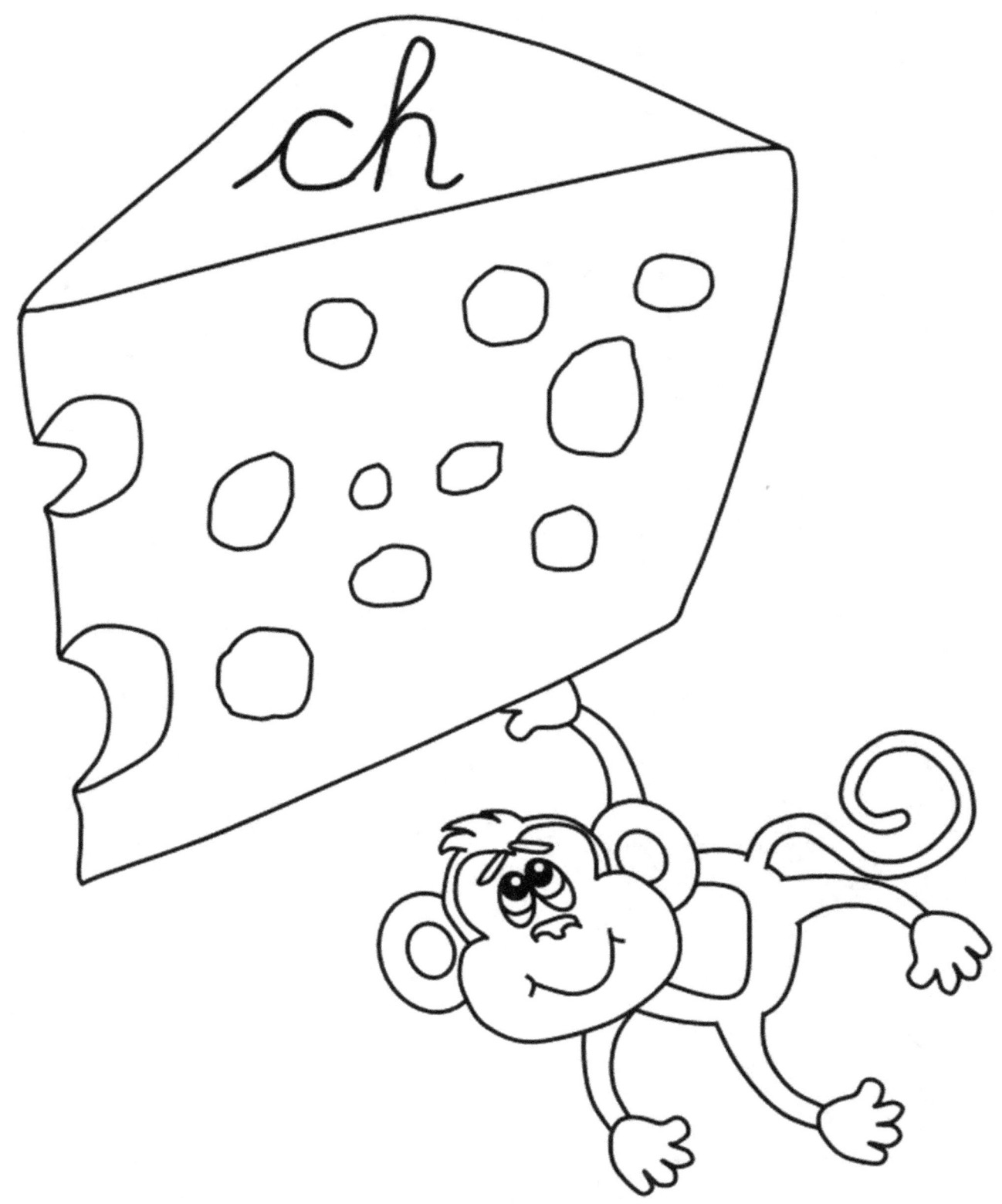

Trace the steps for making the letter c on the following line.

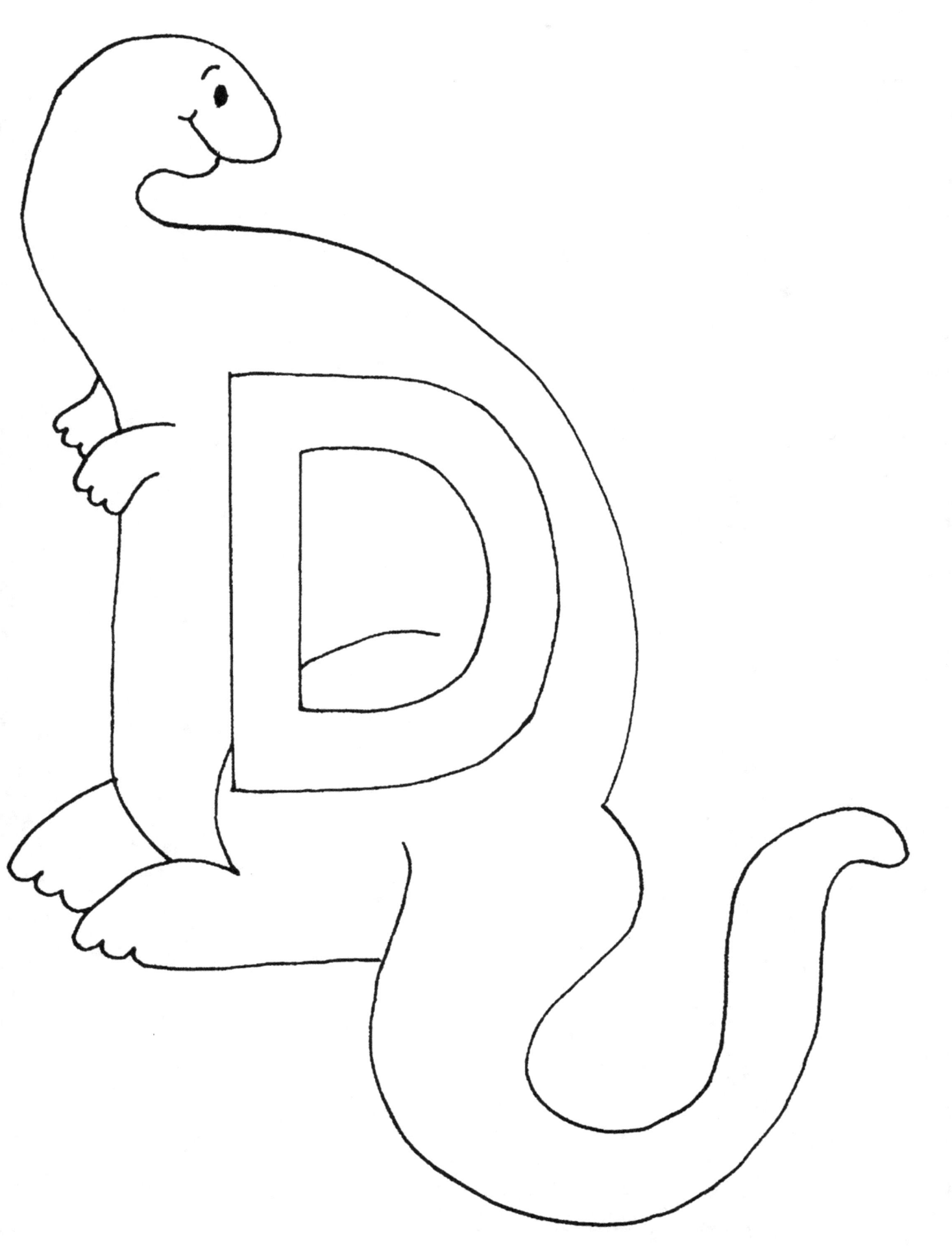

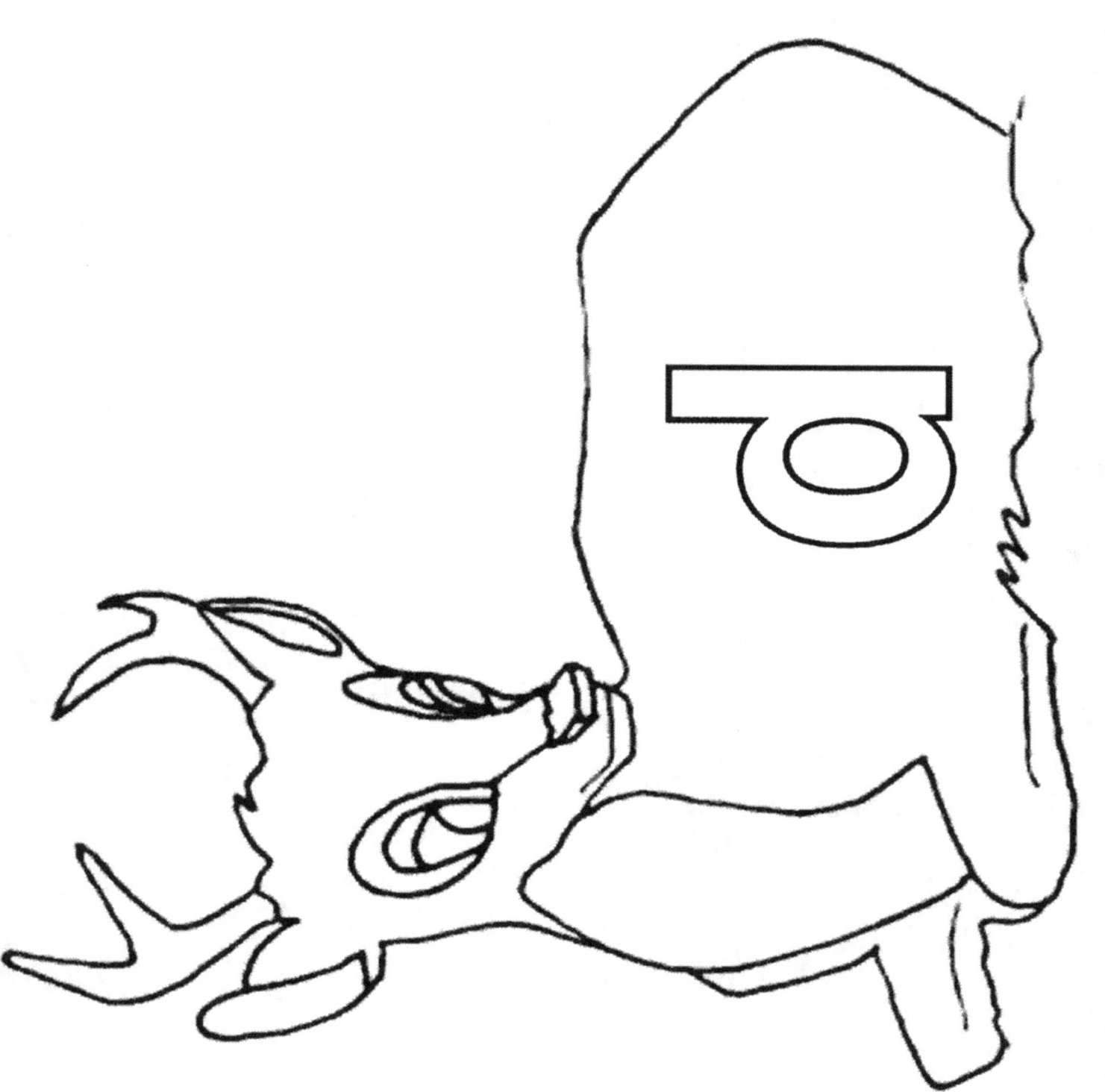

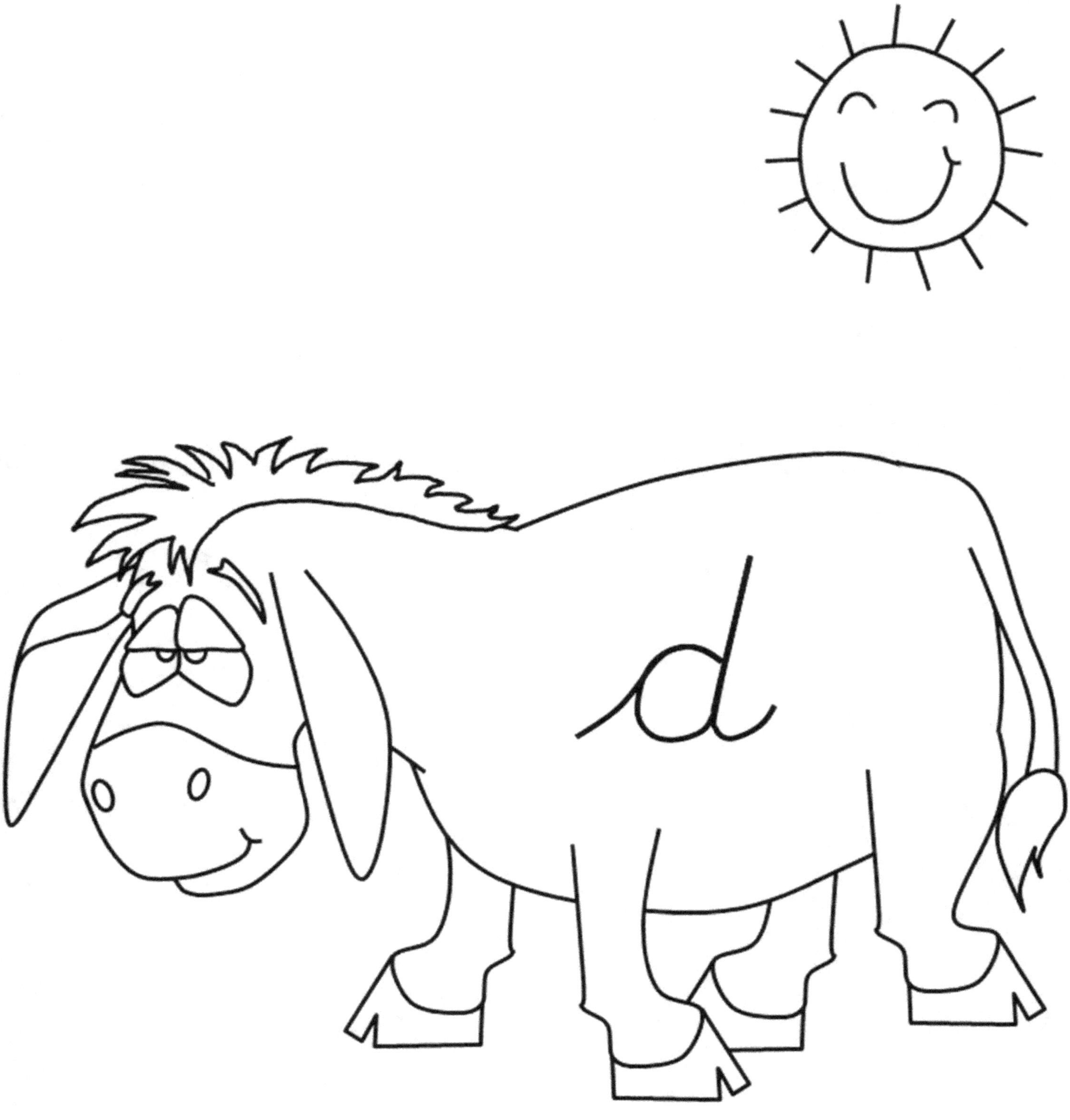

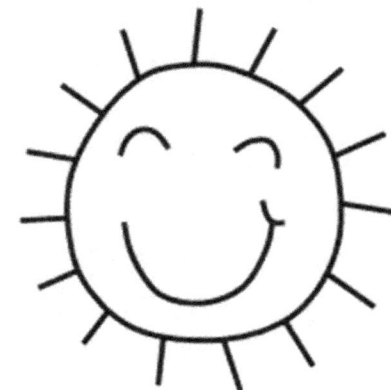

Trace the steps for making the letter d on the following line.

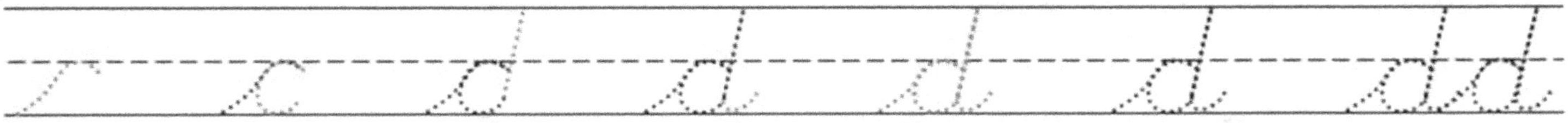

d   d   d   d   d   dd

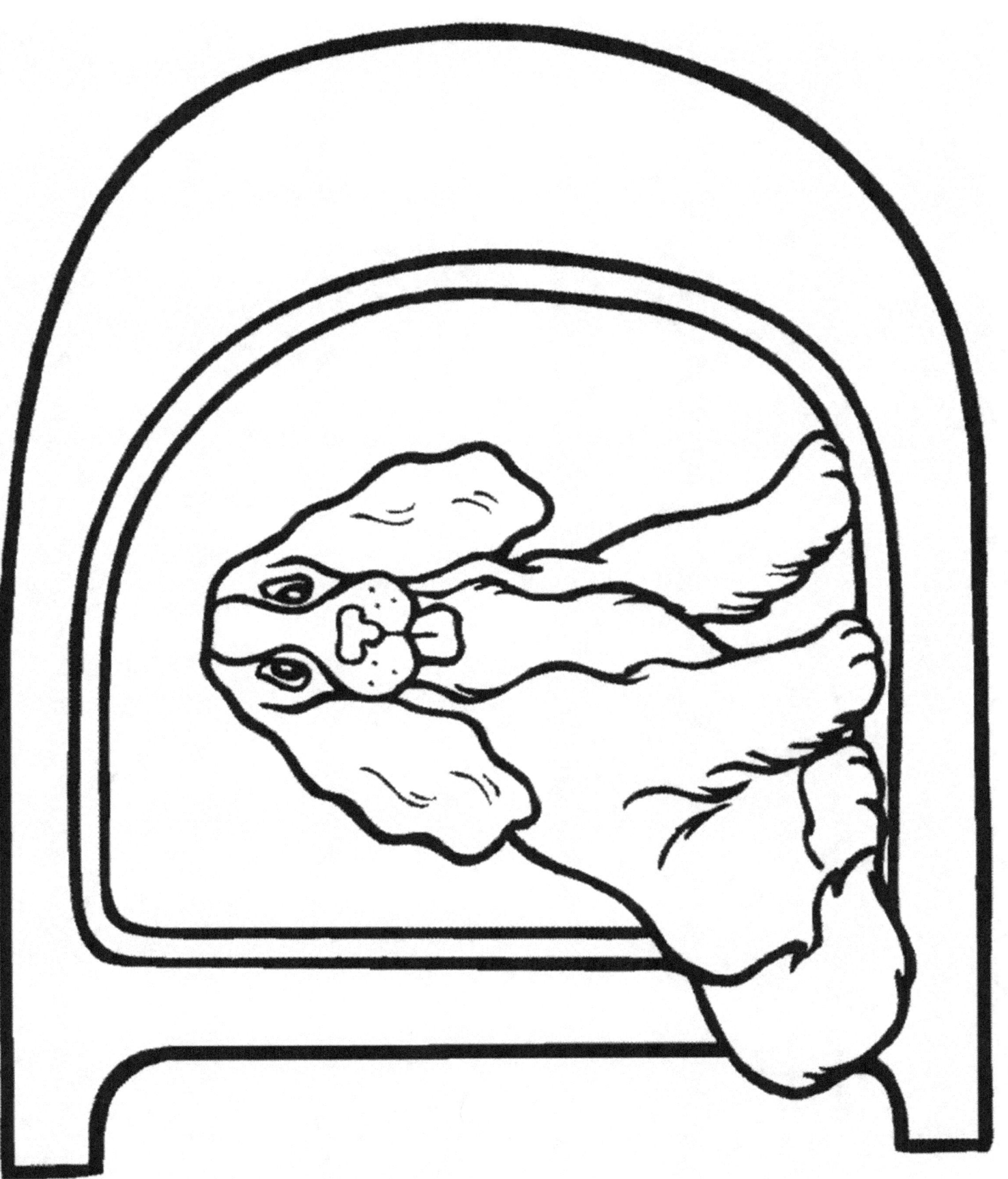

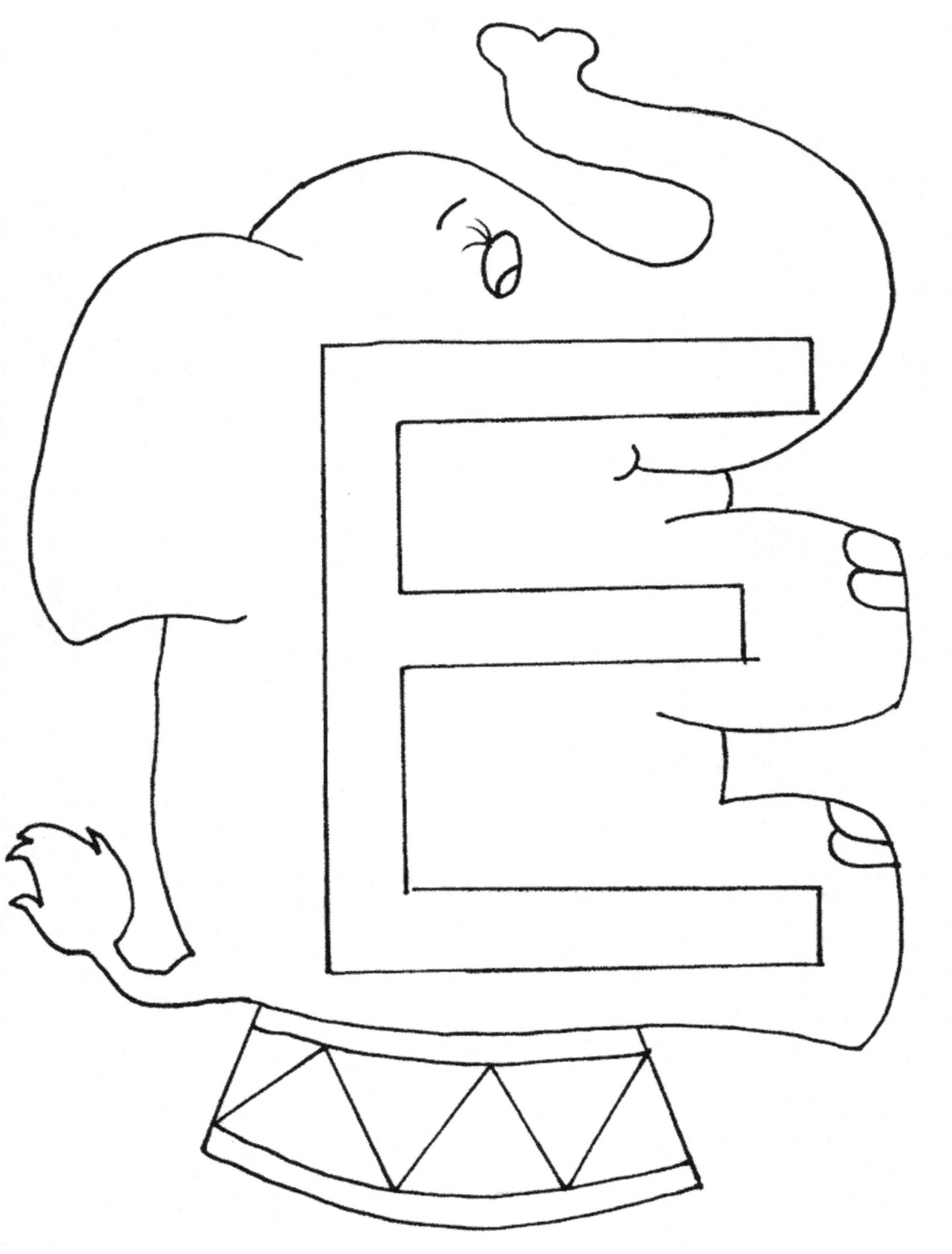

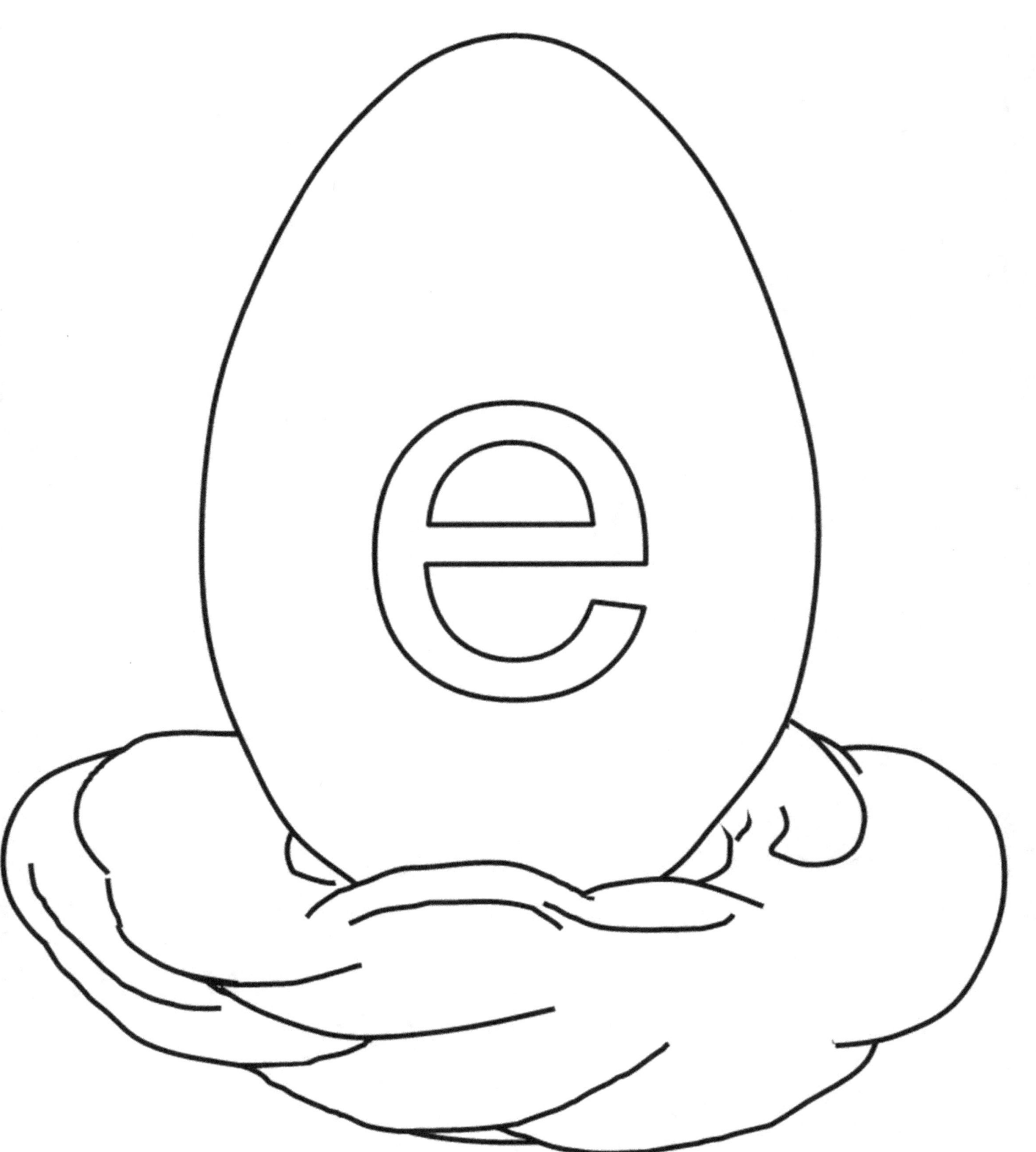

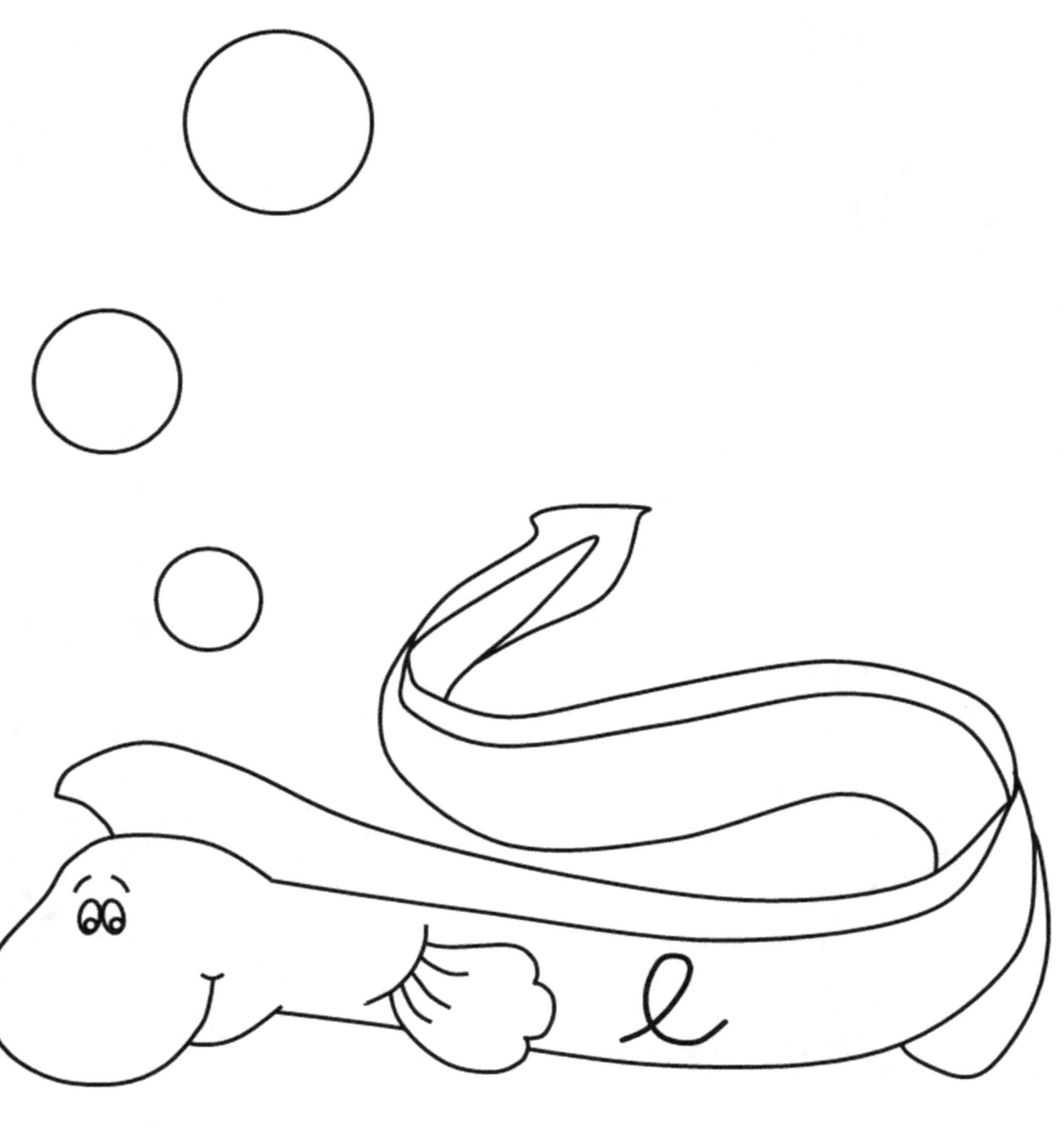

Trace the steps for making the letter e on the following line.

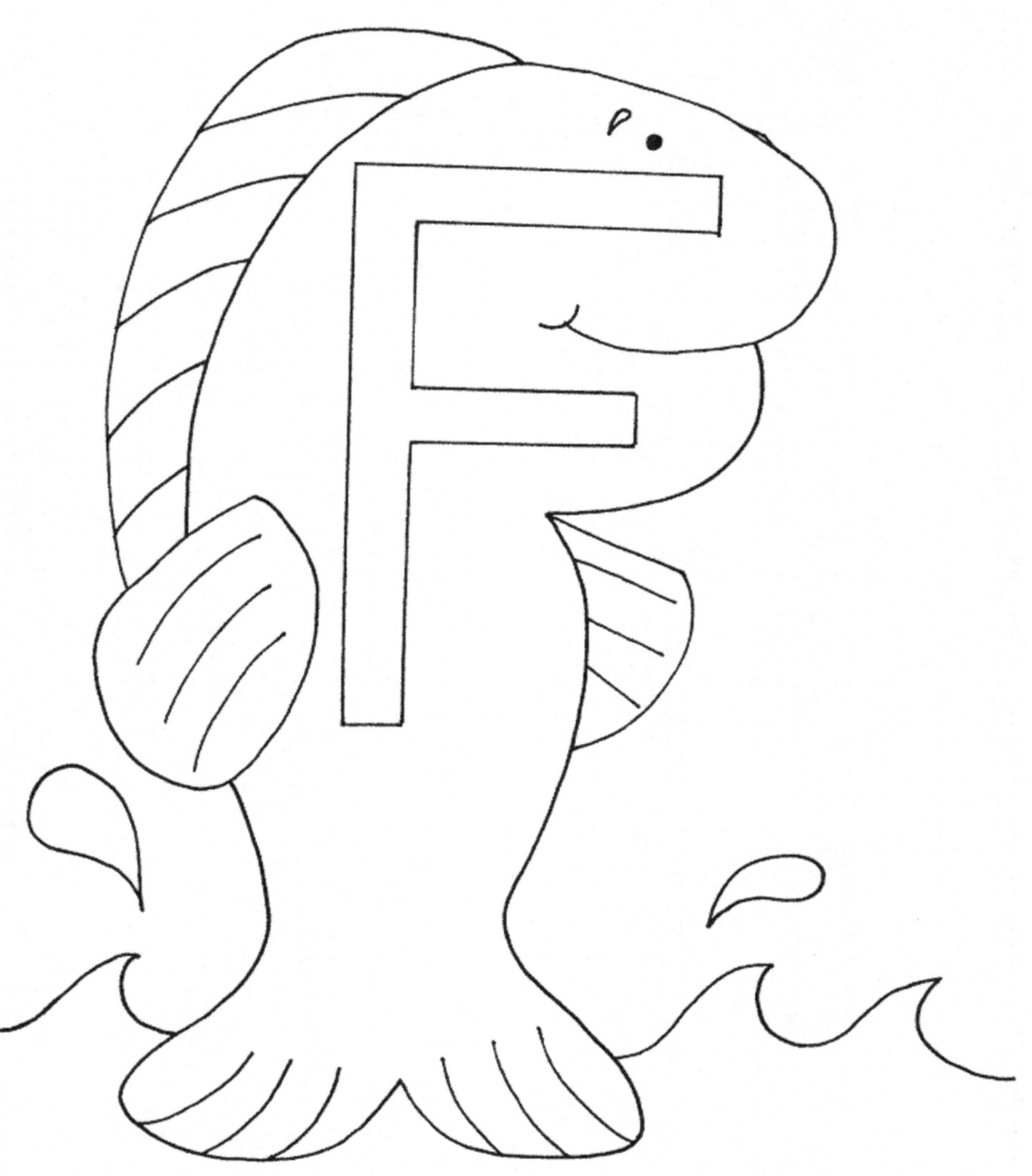

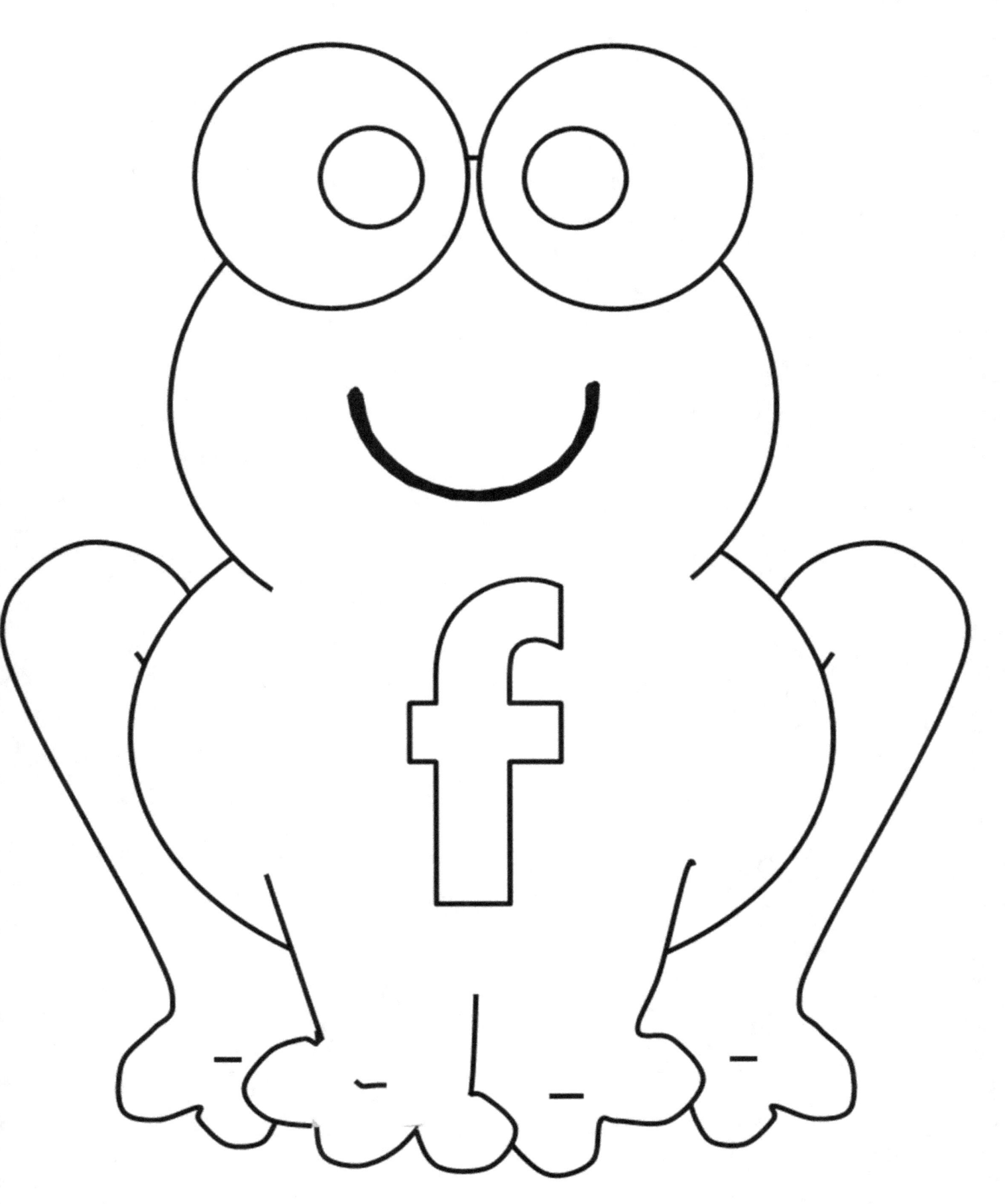

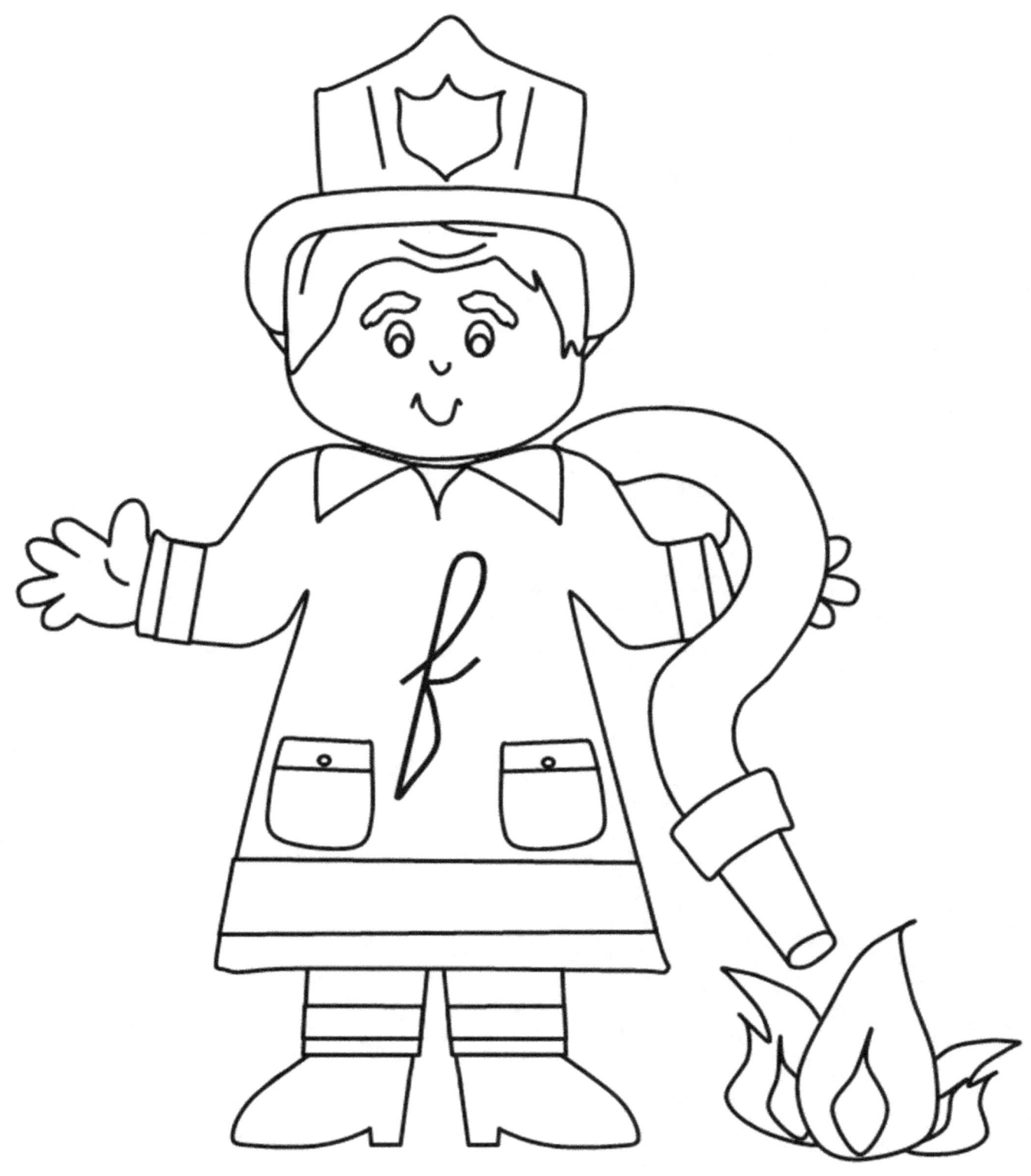

Trace the steps for making the letter f on the following line.

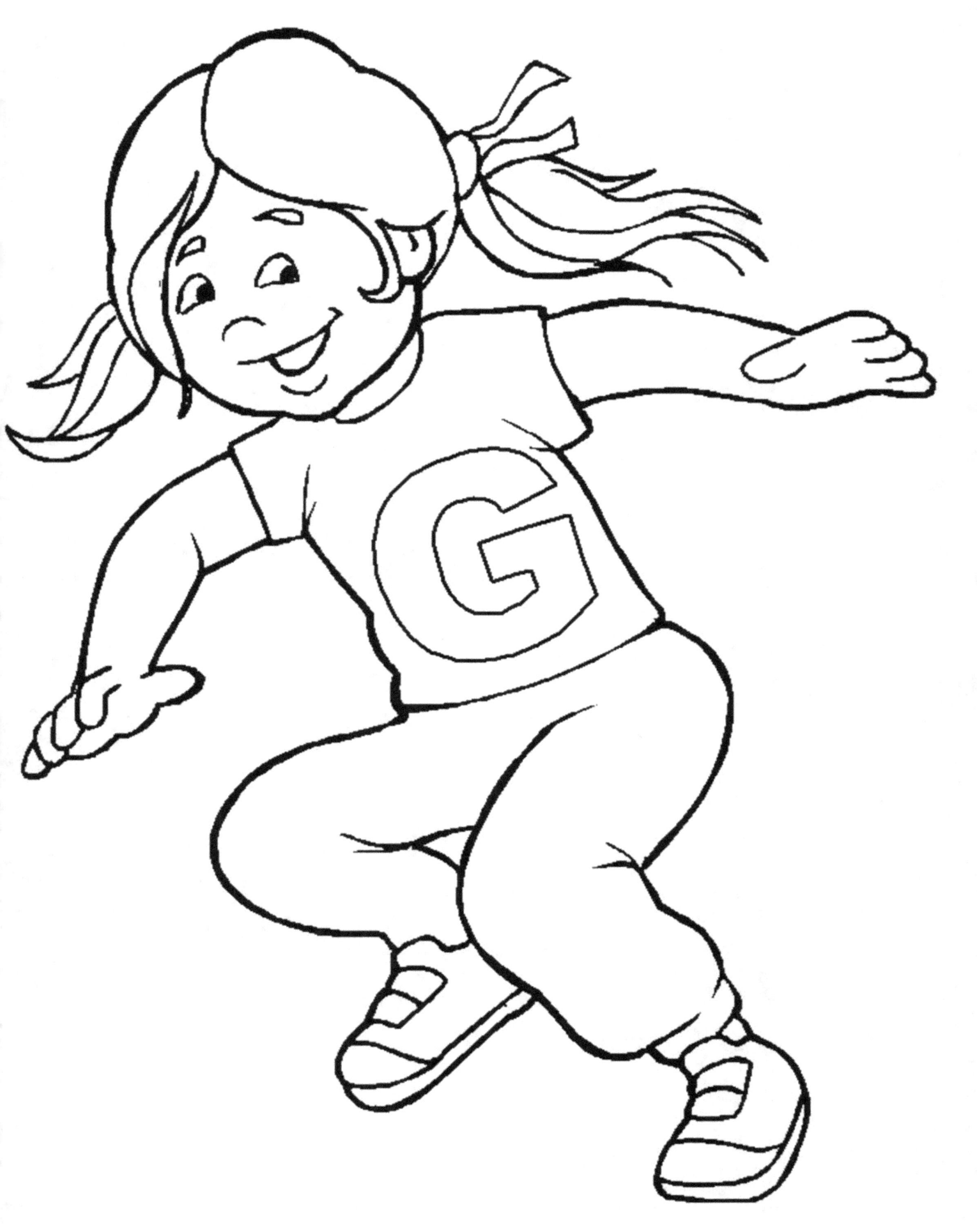

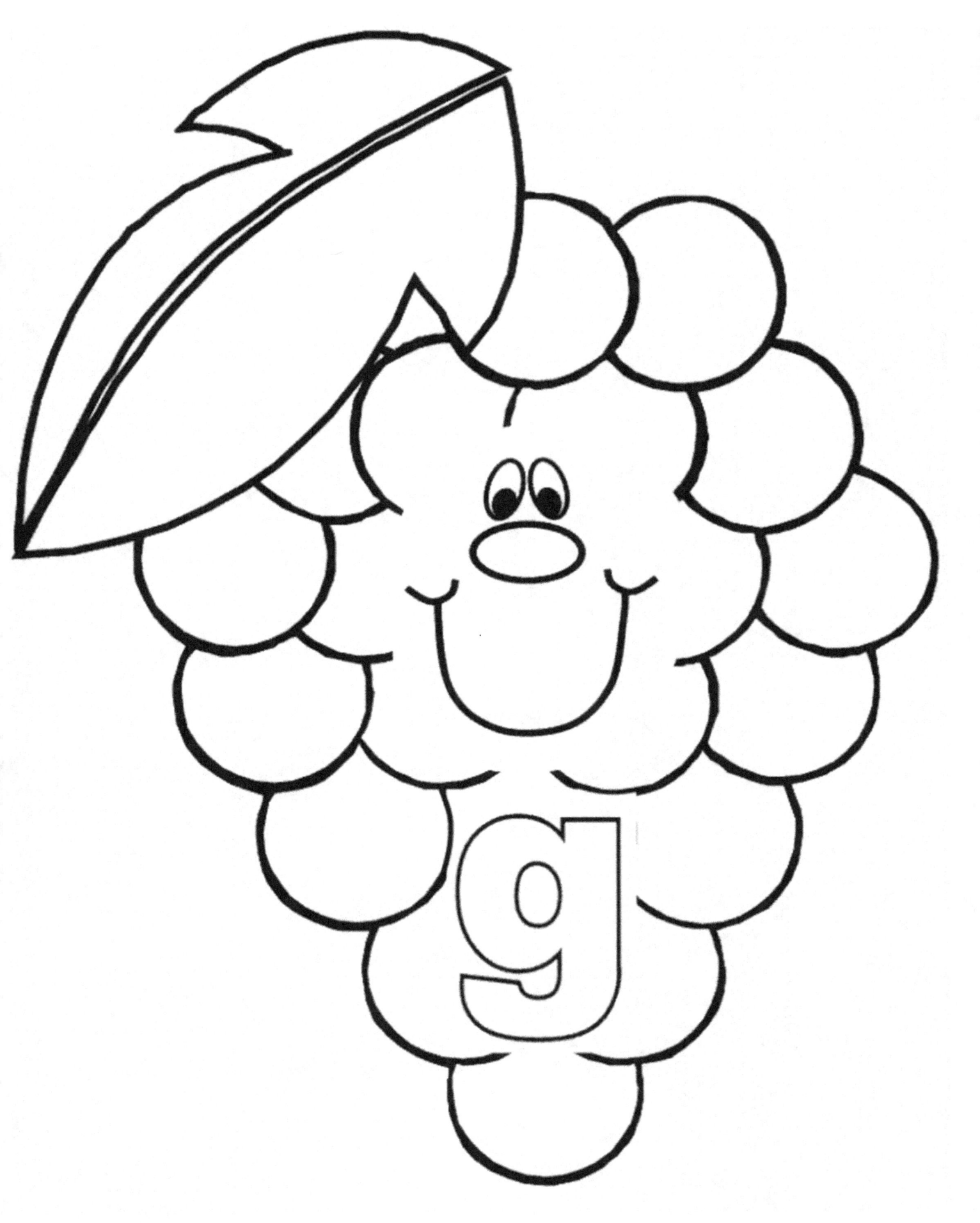

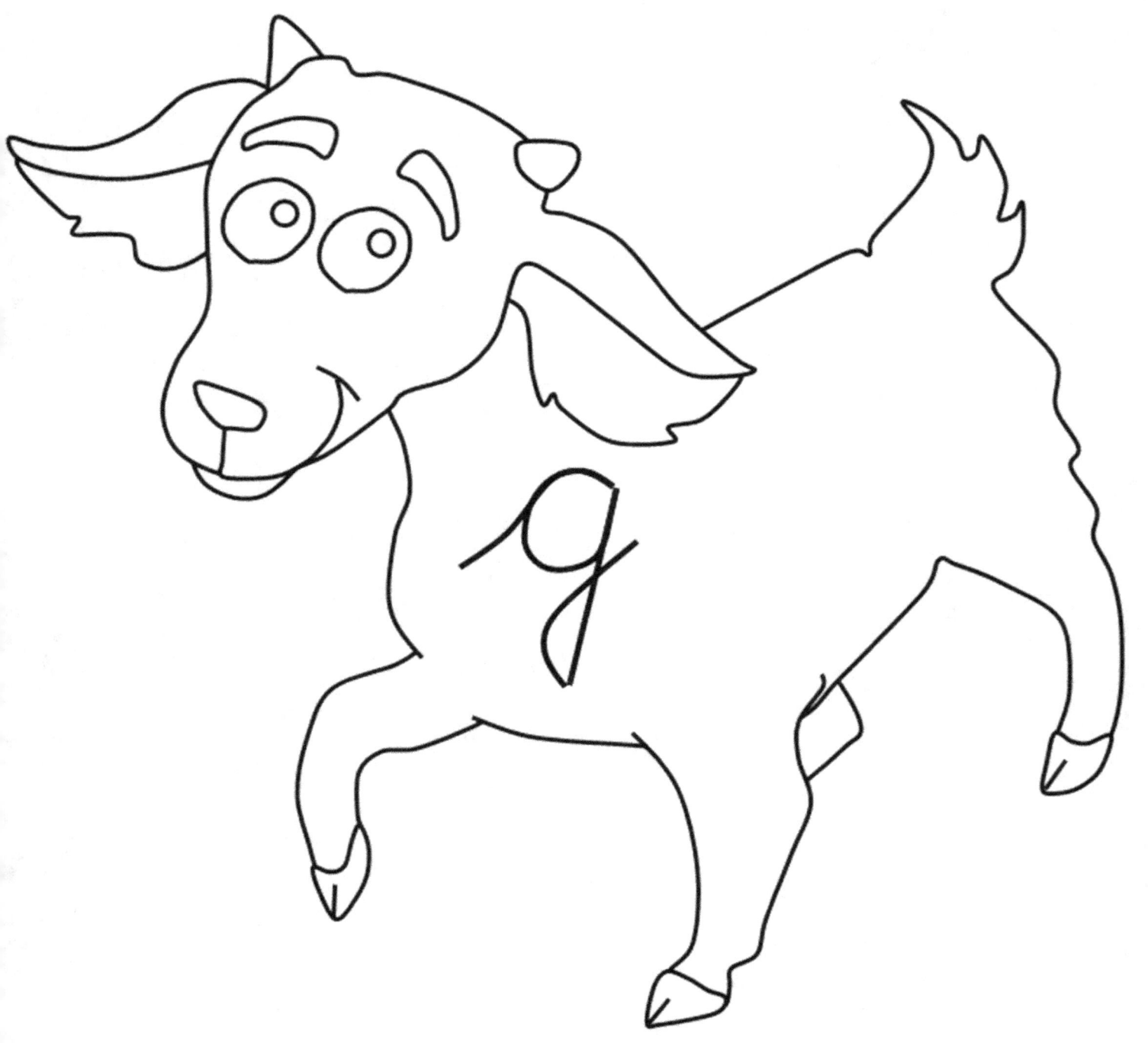

Trace the steps for making the letter g on the following line.

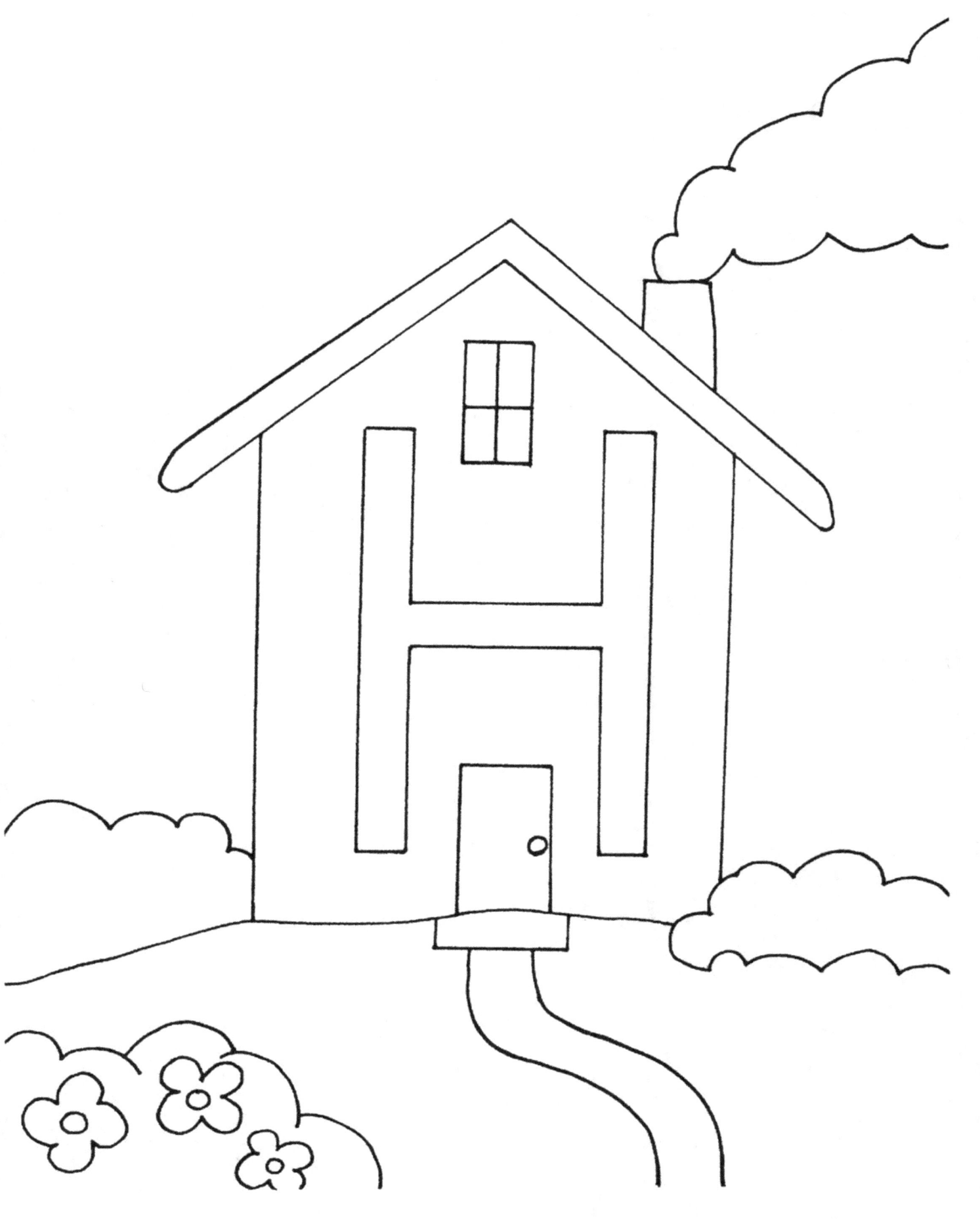

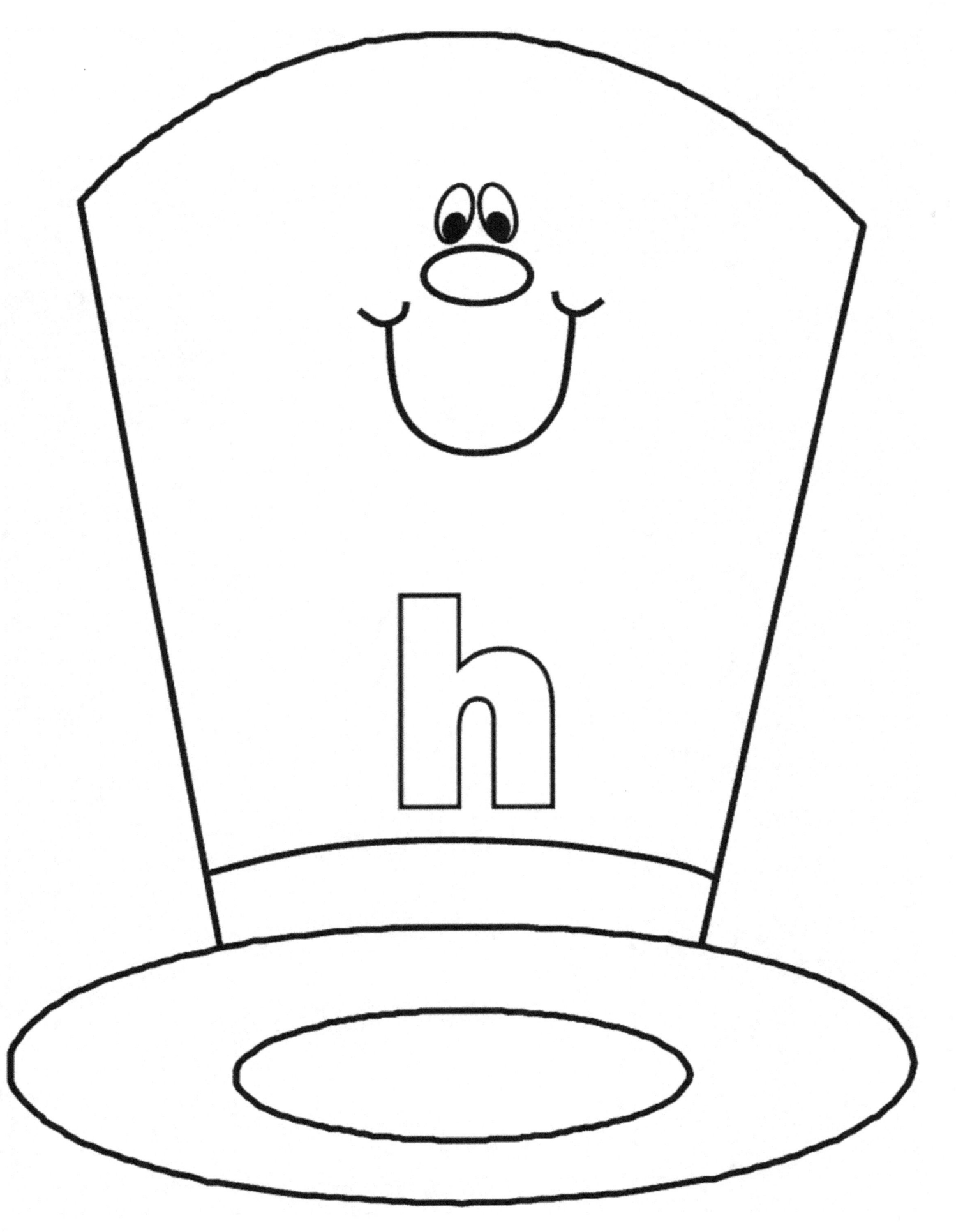

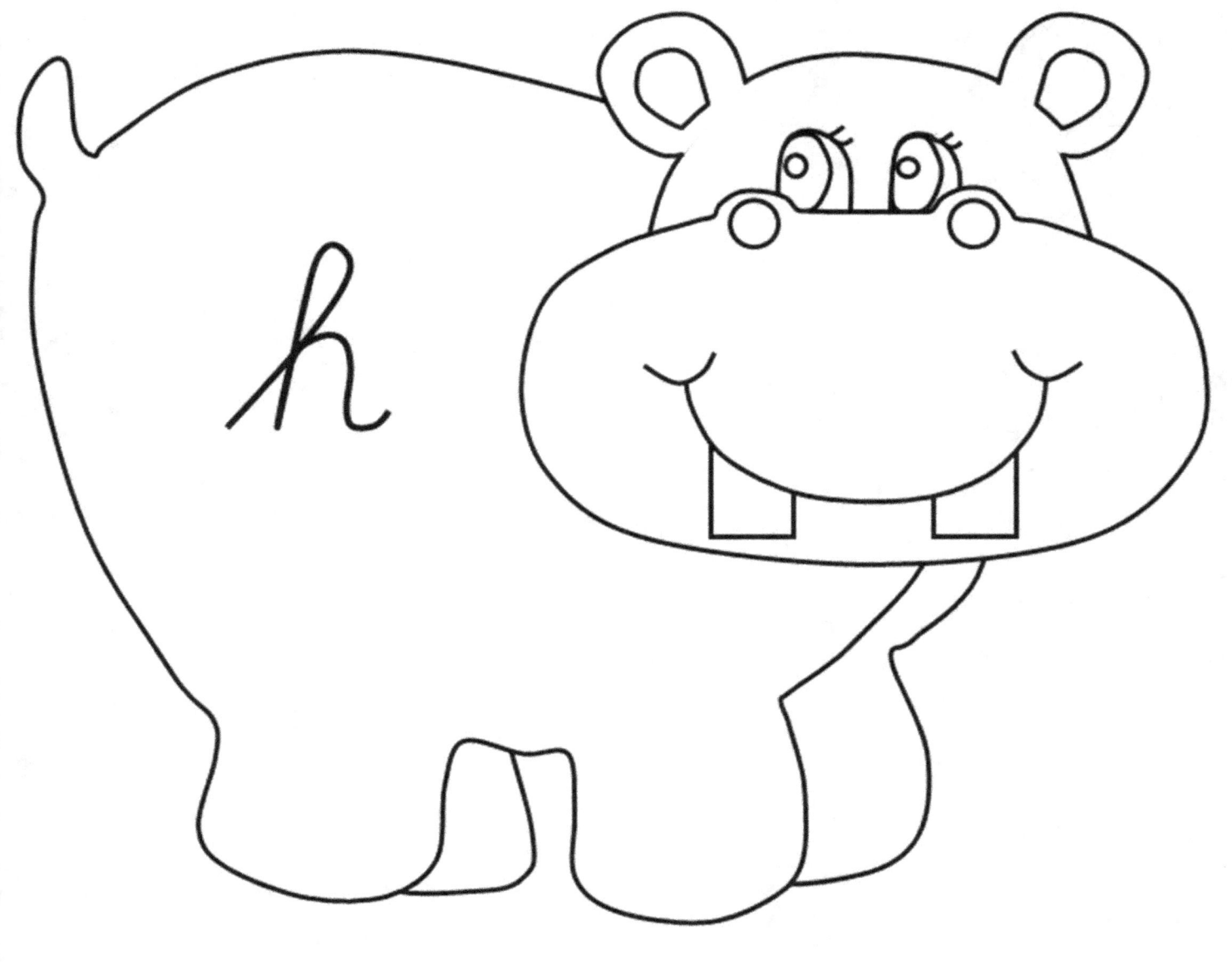

Trace the steps for making the letter h on the following line.

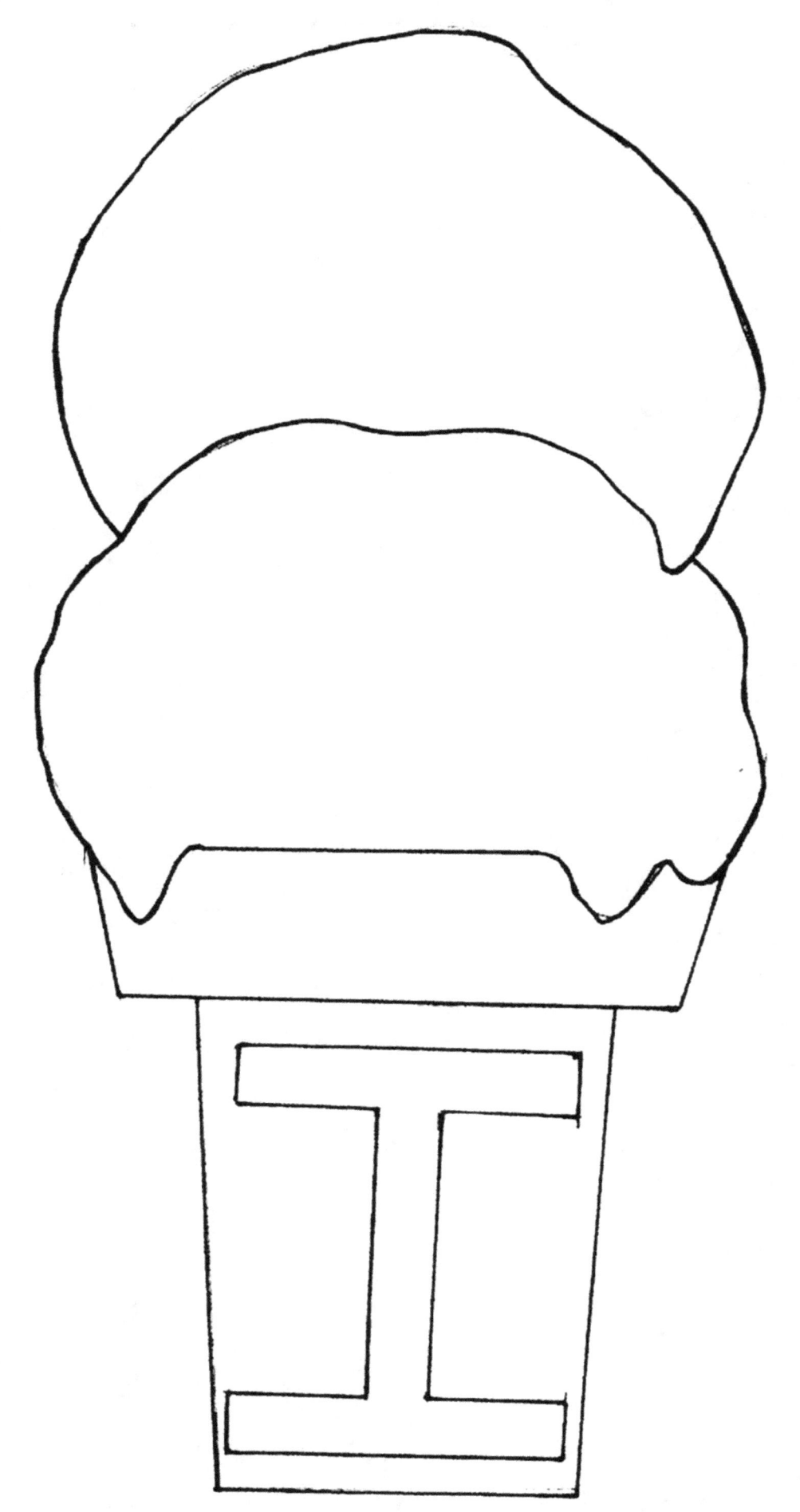

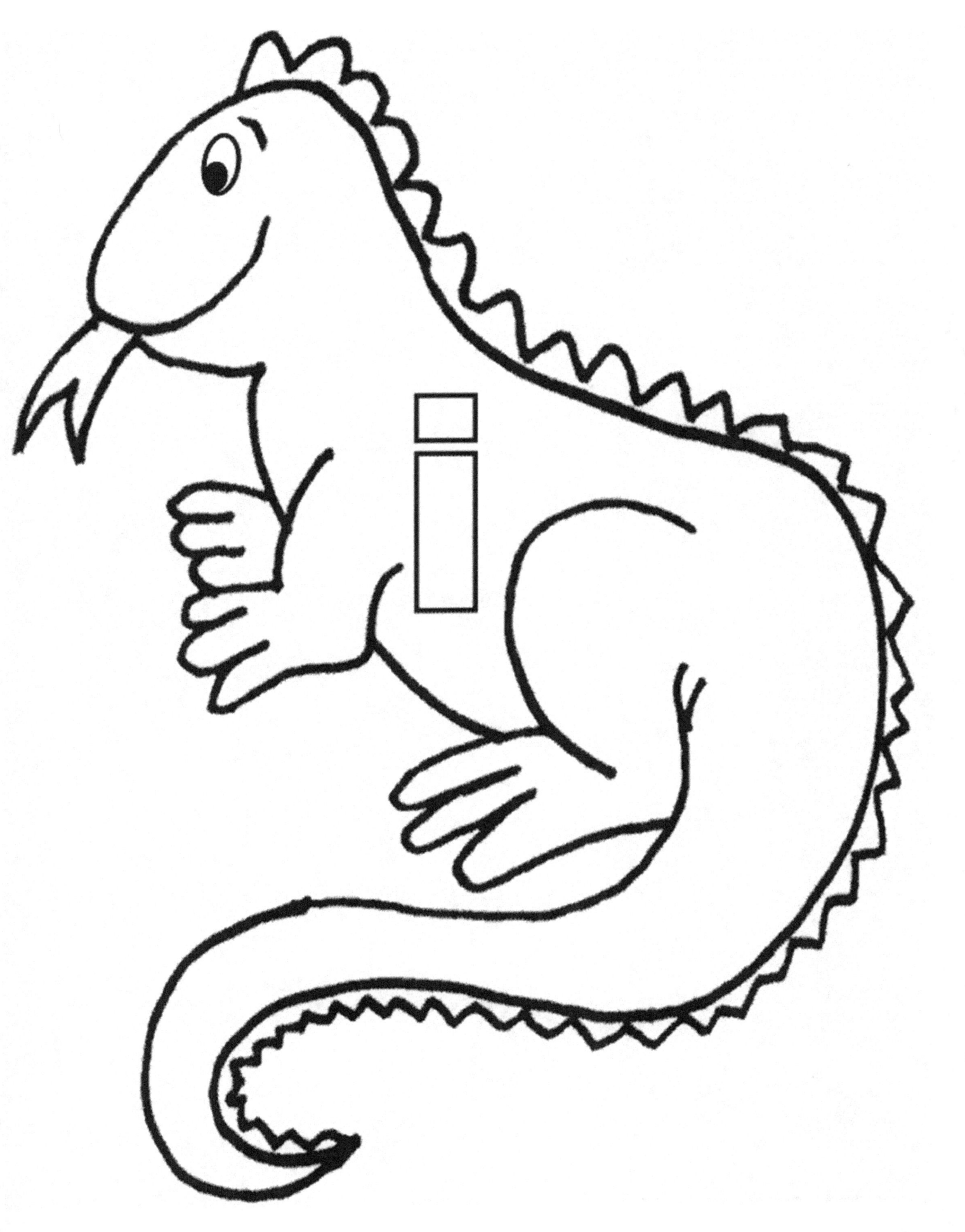

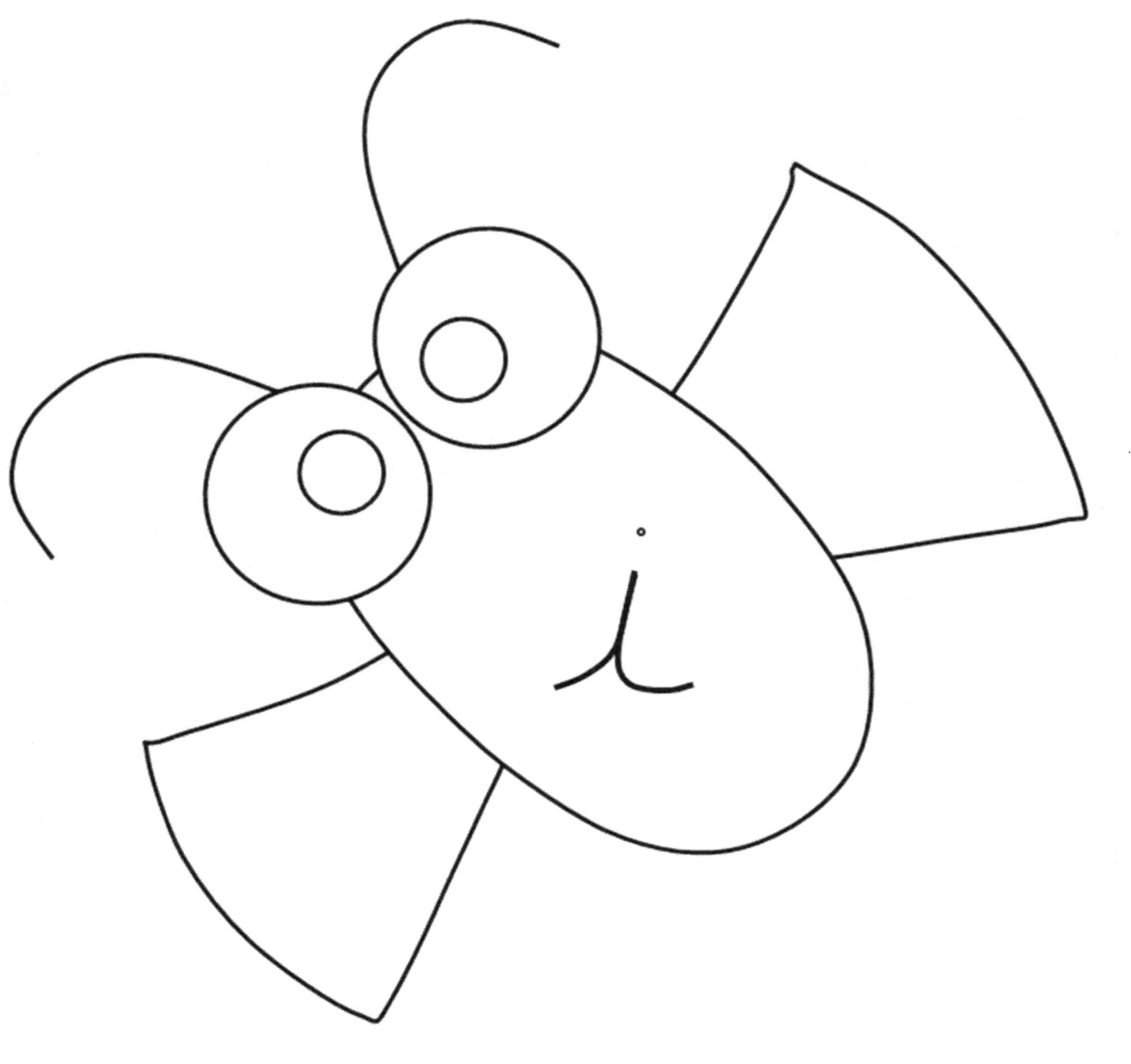

Trace the steps for making the letter i on the following line.

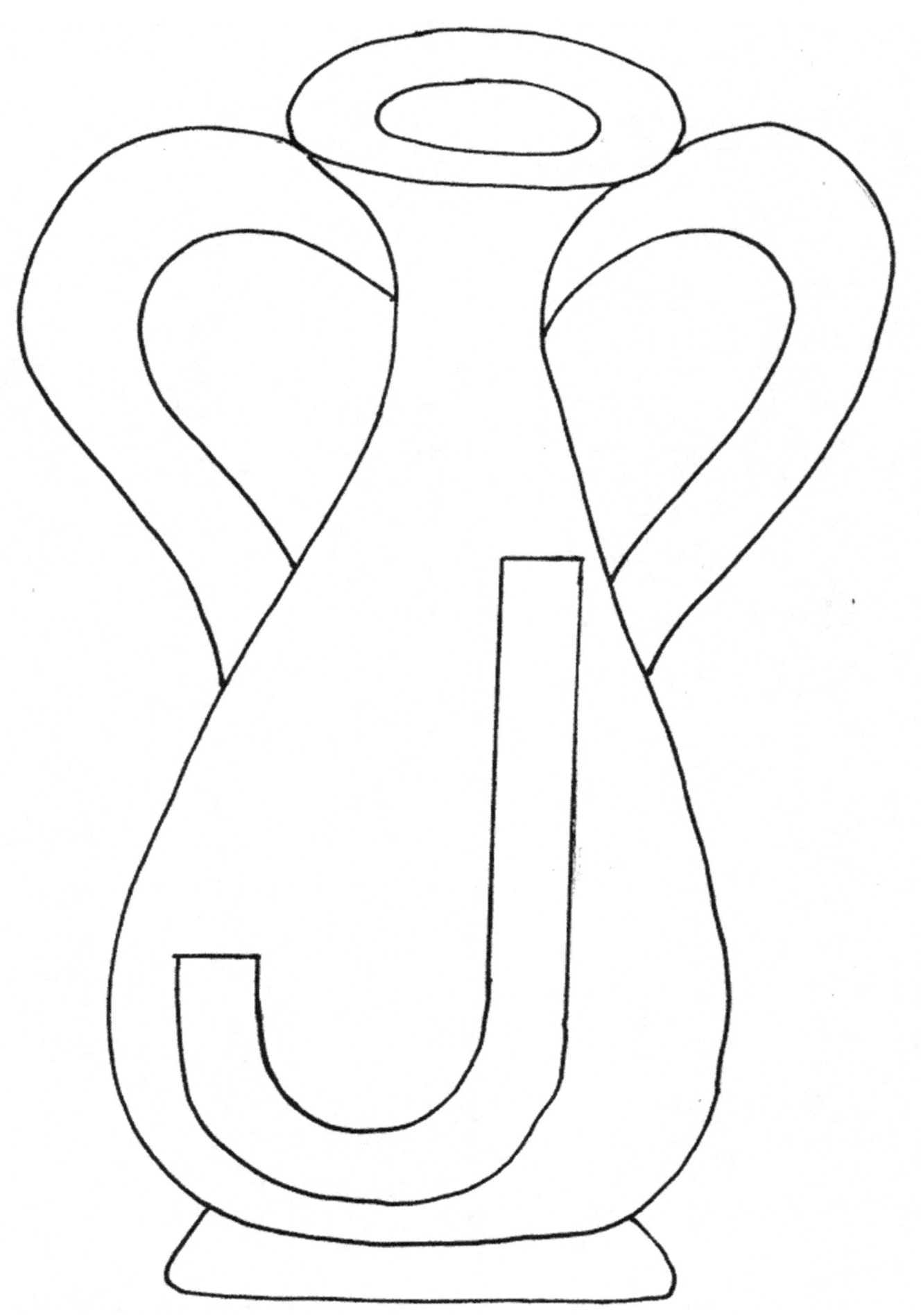

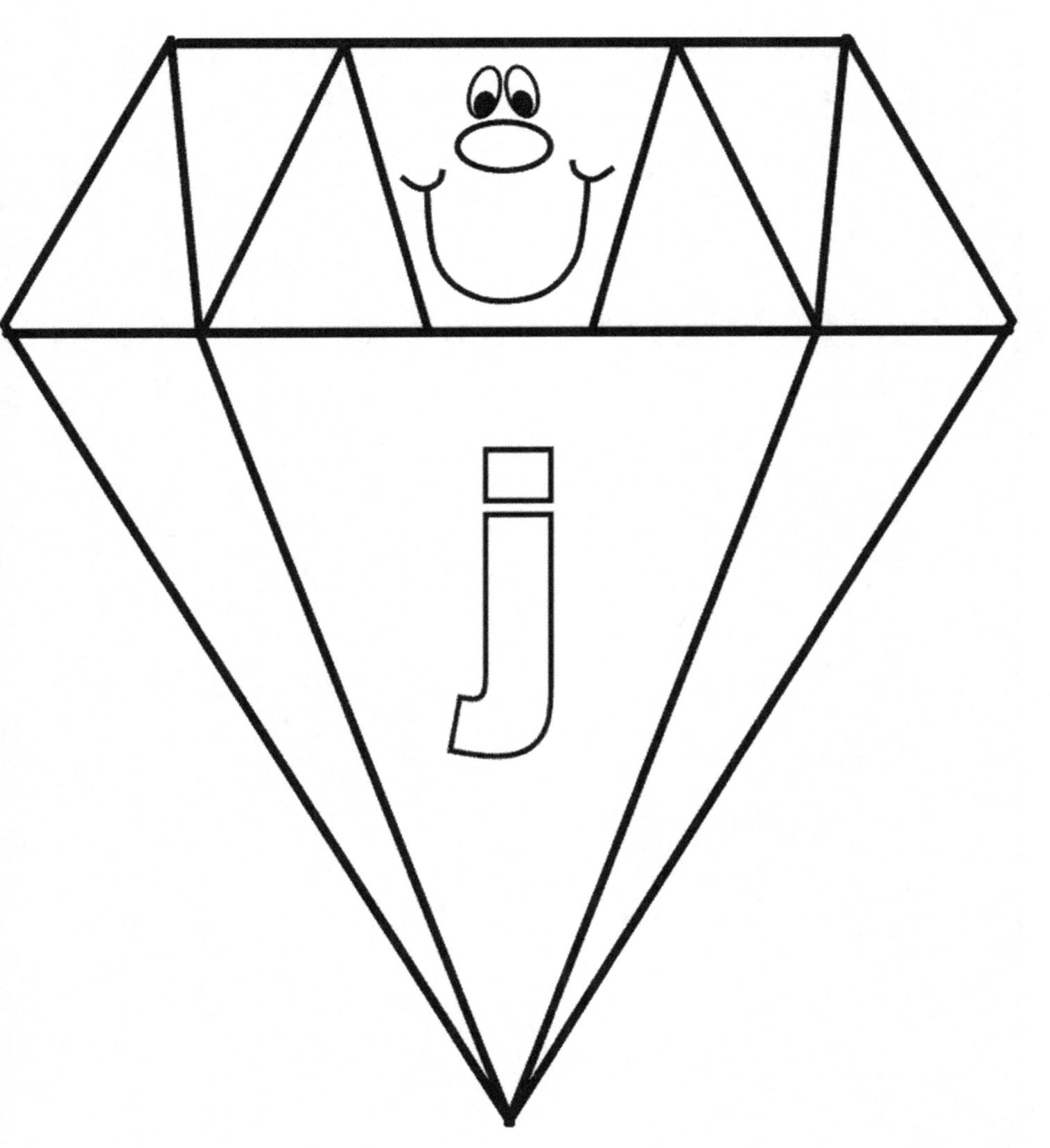

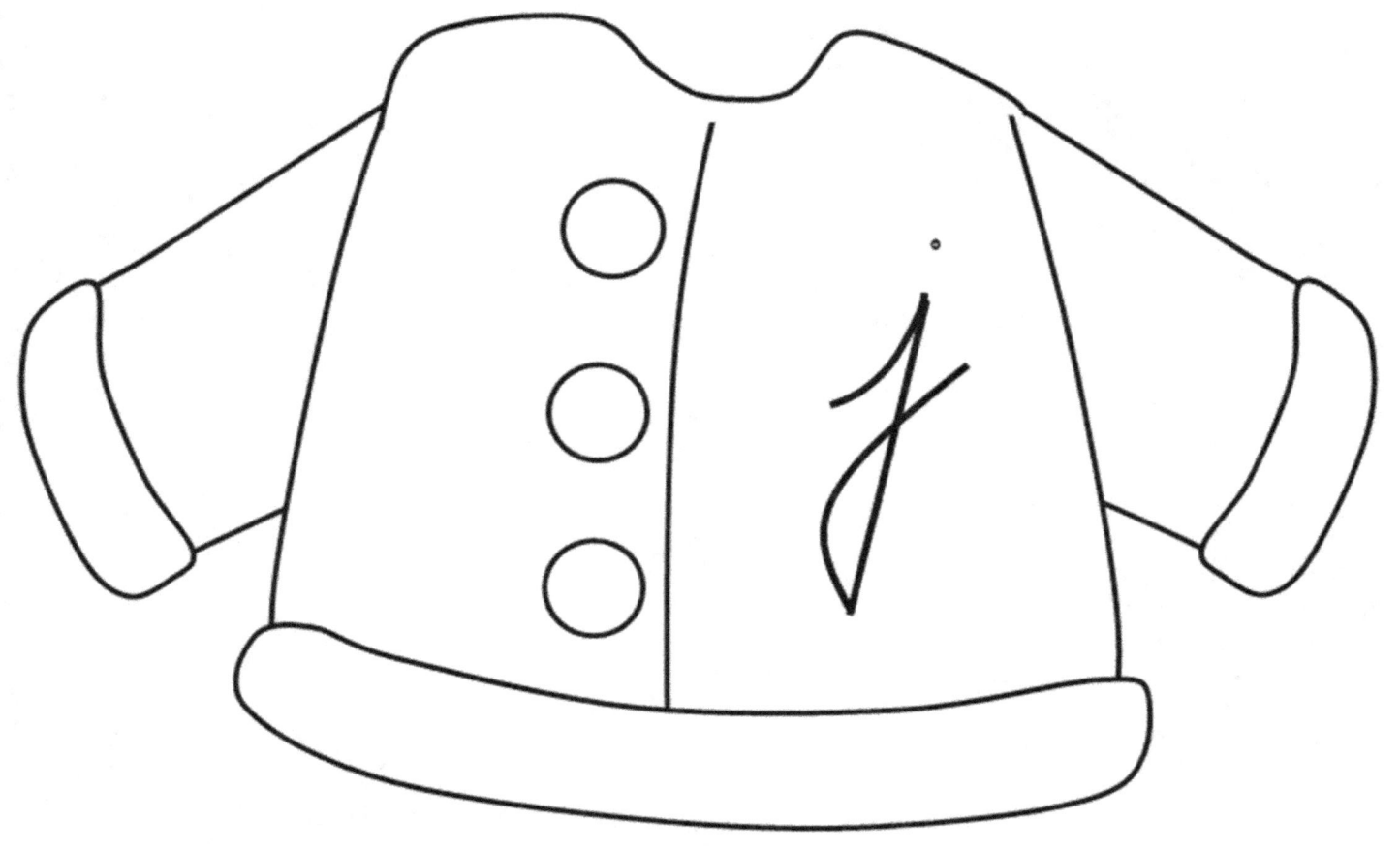

Trace the steps for making the letter j on the following line.

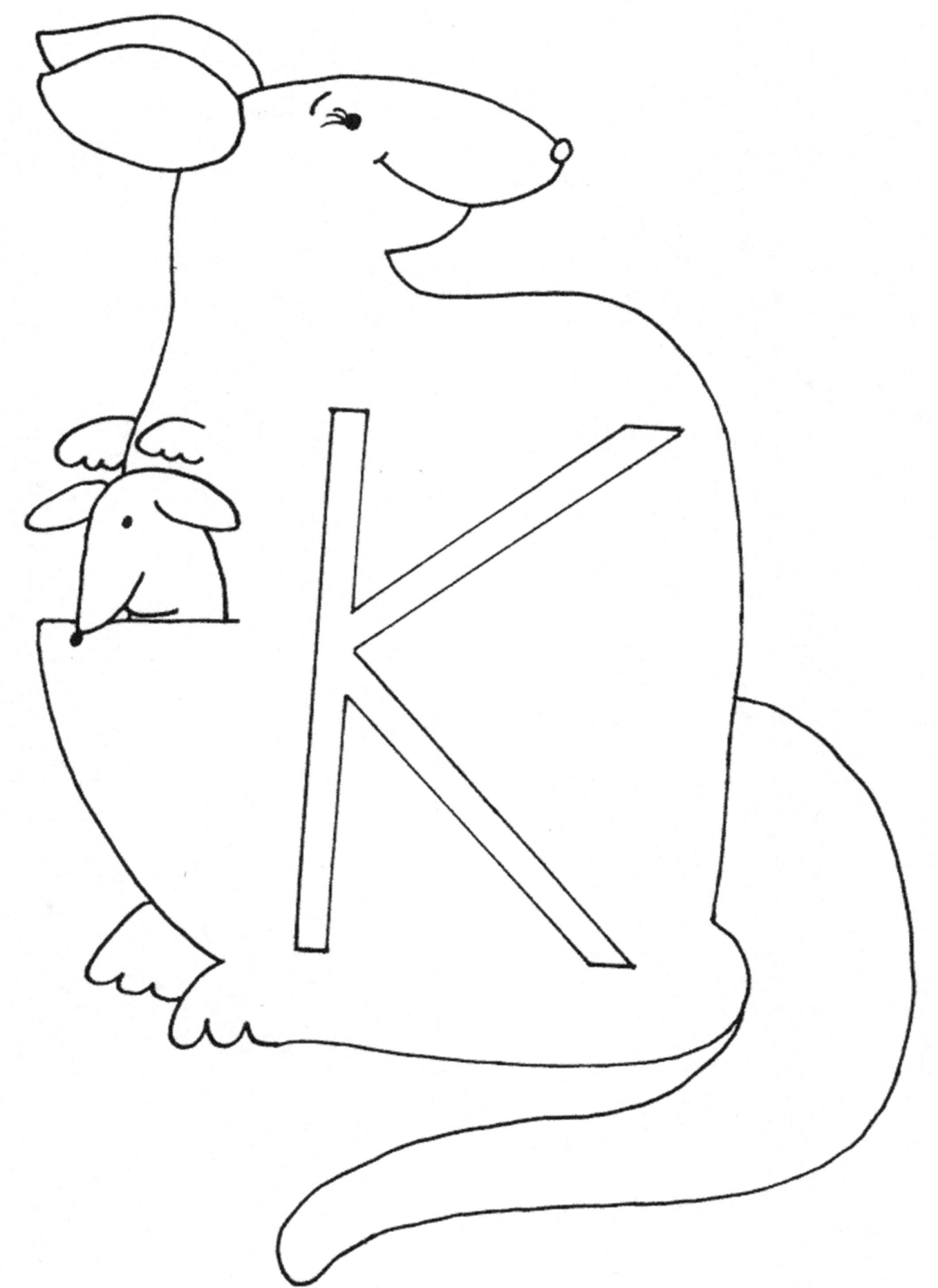

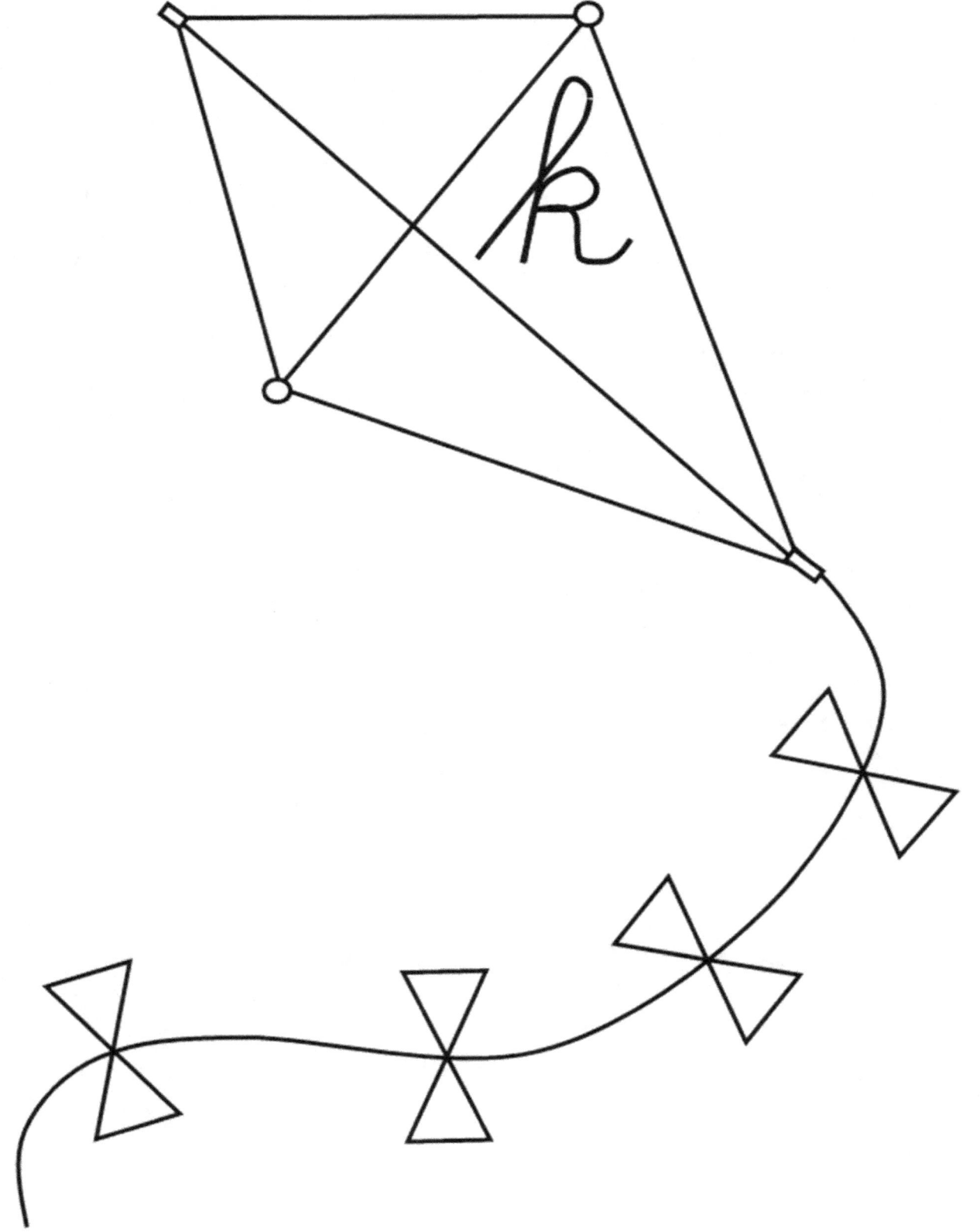

Trace the steps for making the letter k on the following line.

$/ \quad k \quad k \quad k \quad k \quad k \quad kk$

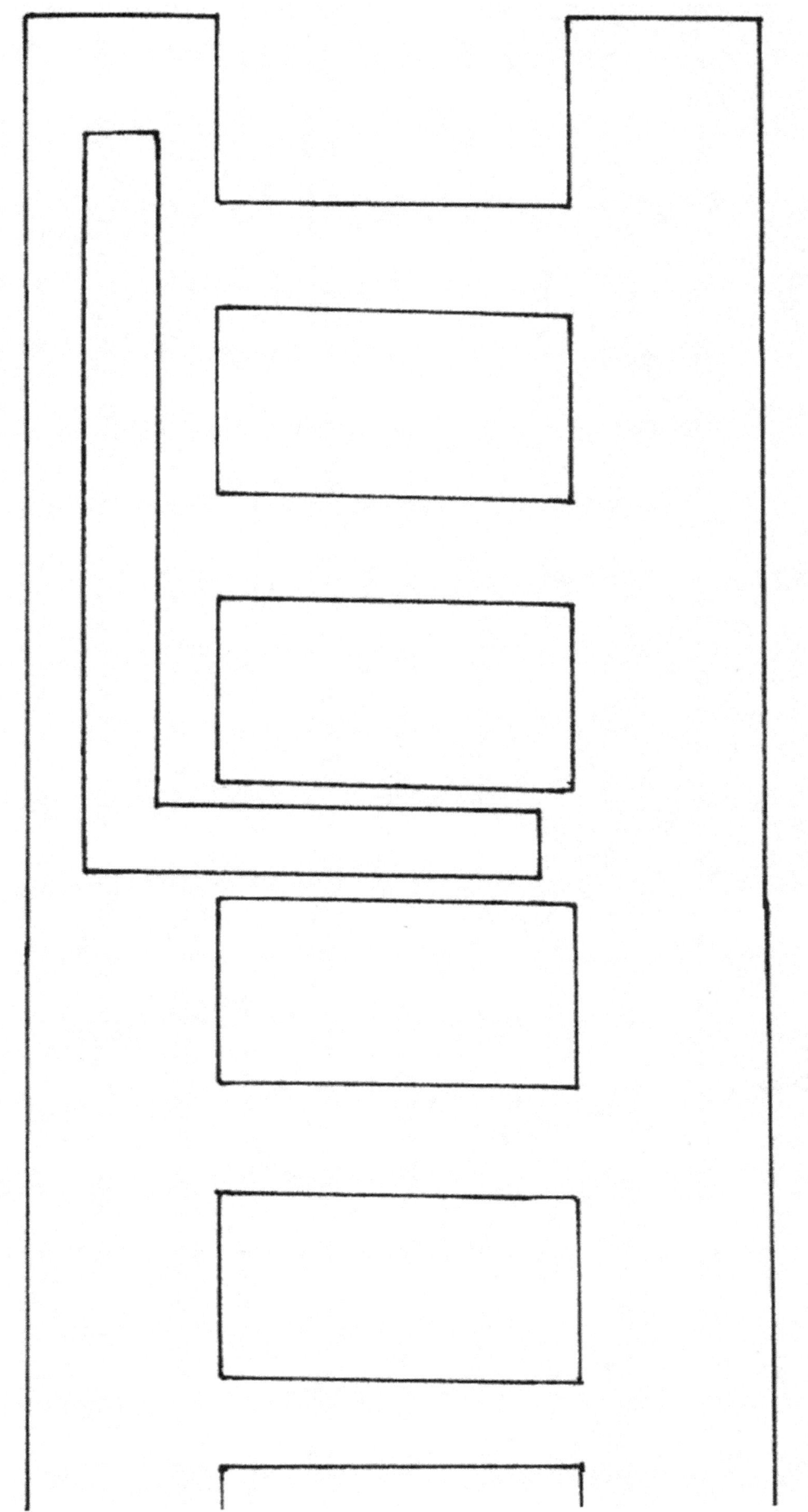

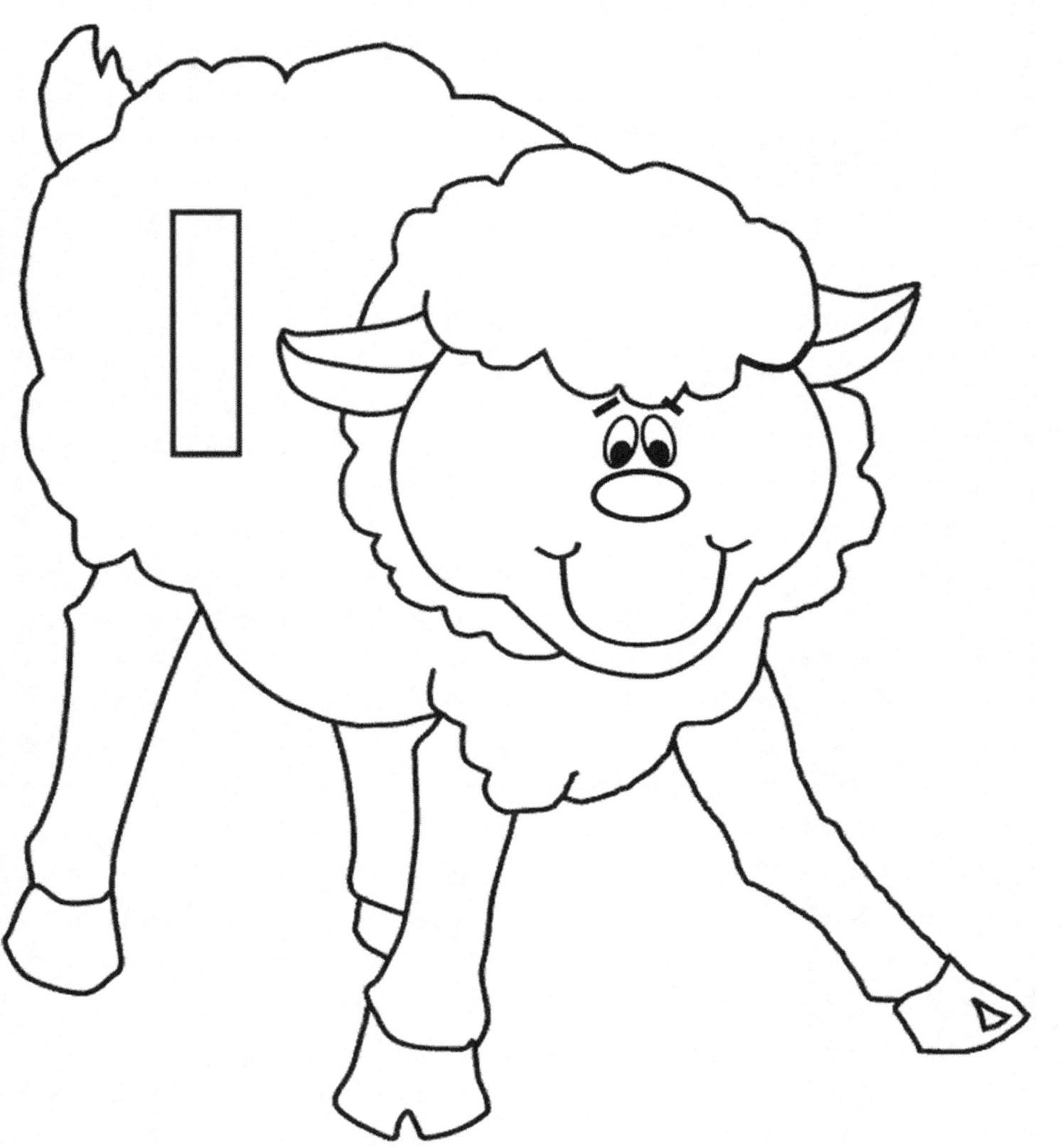

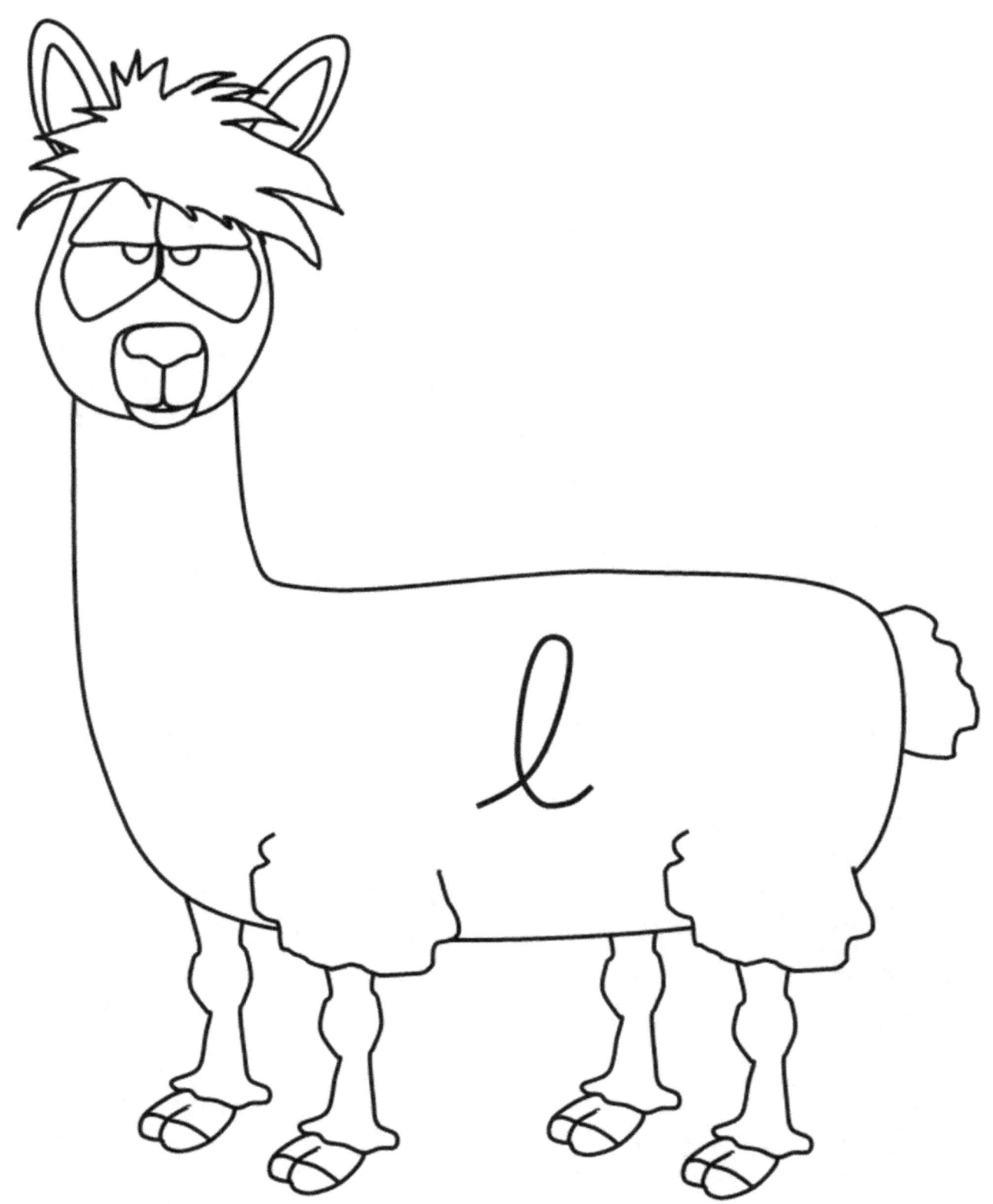

Trace the steps for making the letter l on the following line.

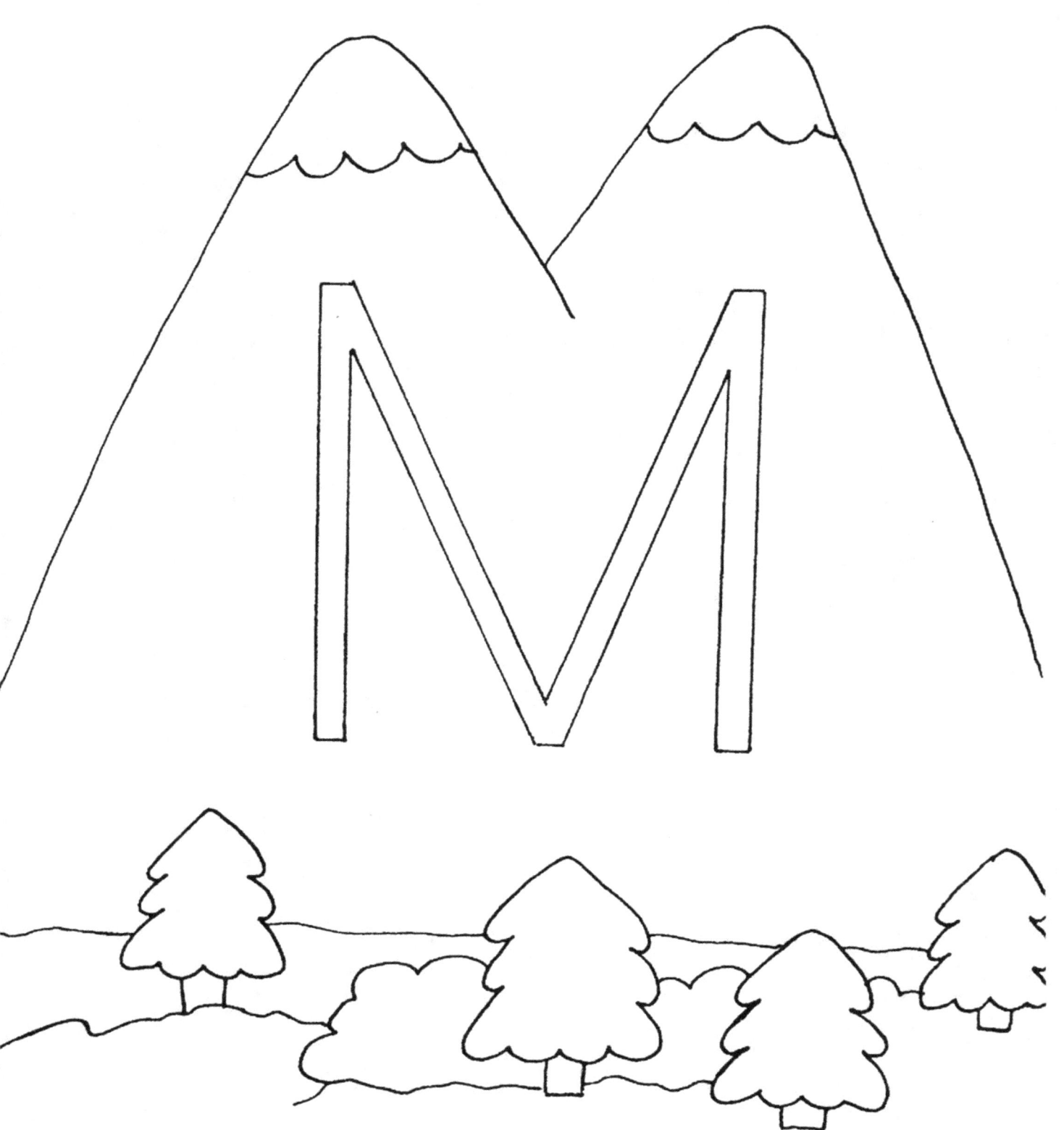

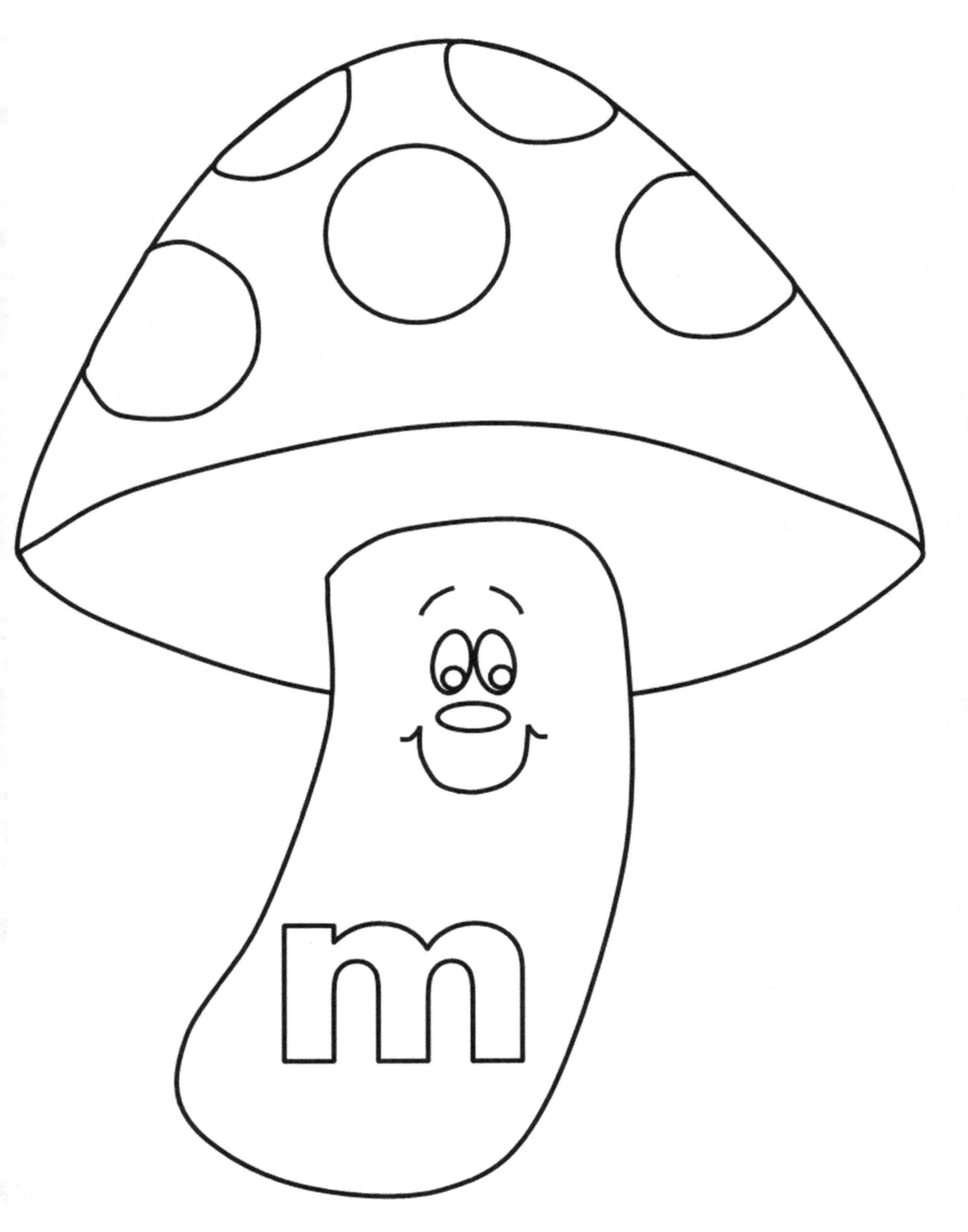

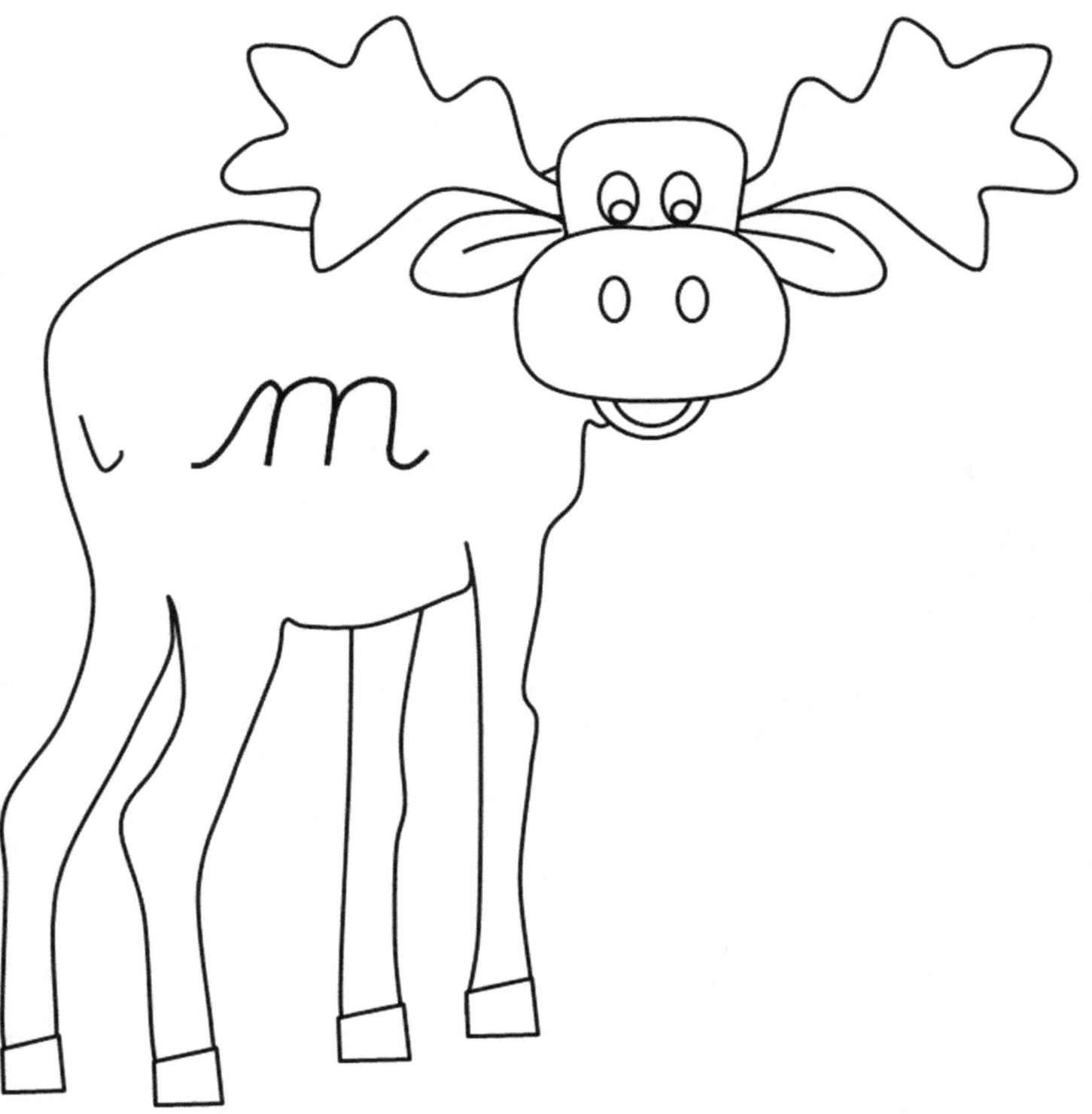

Trace the steps for making the letter m on the following line.

‾‾

⌐ ‿ ‿ ⌐⌐ ‿ ‿ ⌐⌐ ‿ ‿ ⌐⌐ ‿ ‿ ⌐⌐ ‿ ‿ ⌐⌐ ‿ ‿

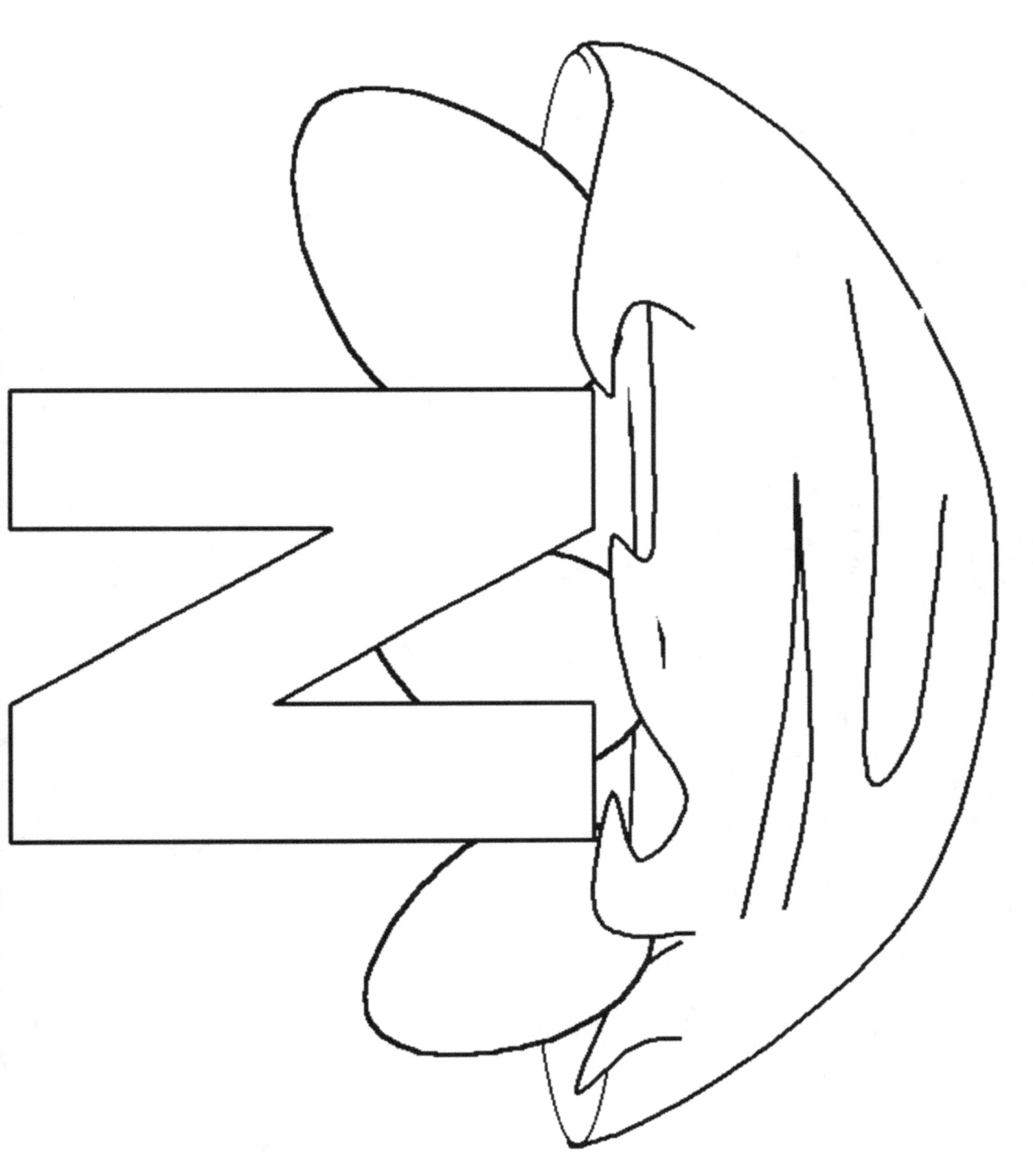

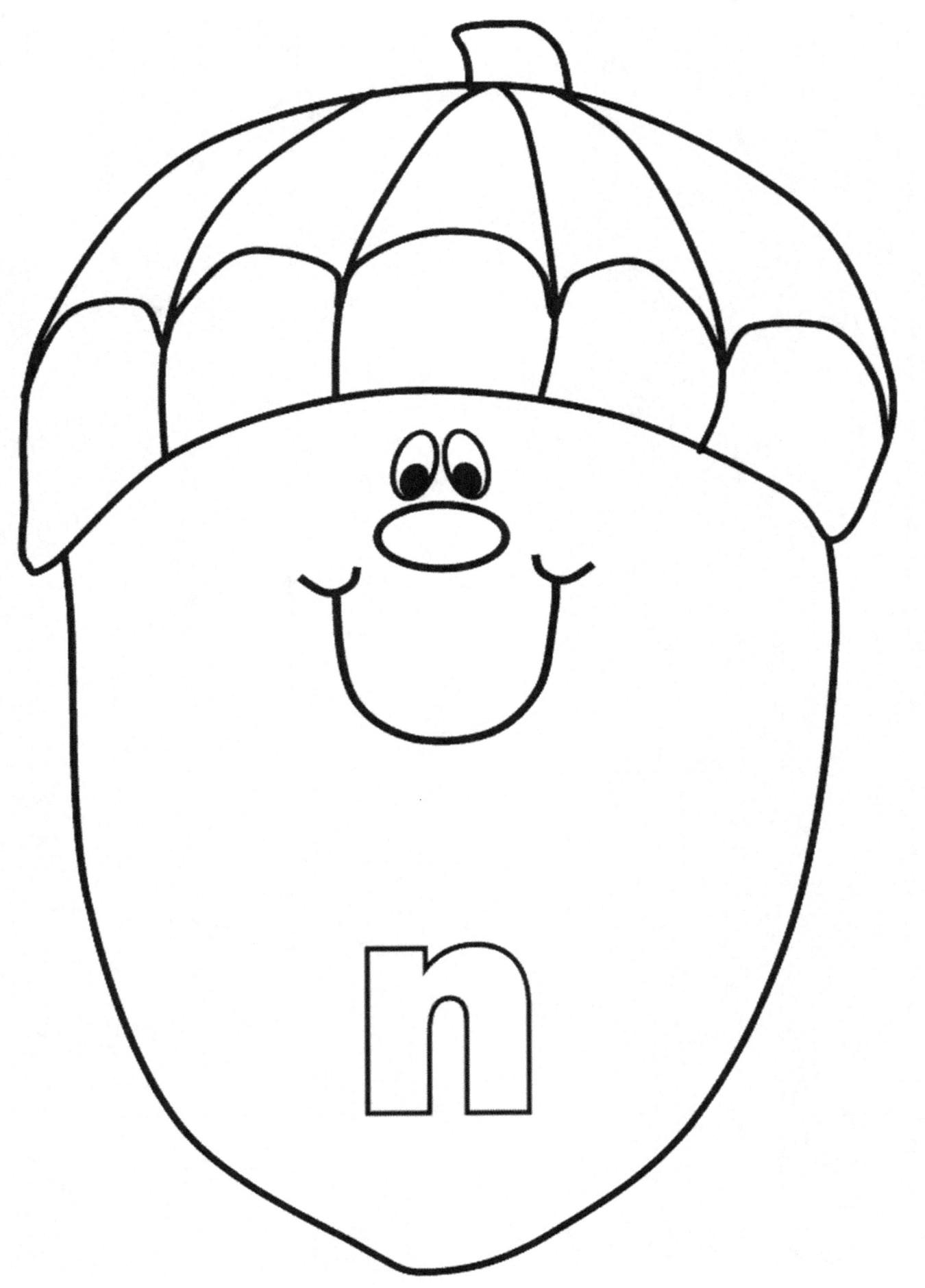

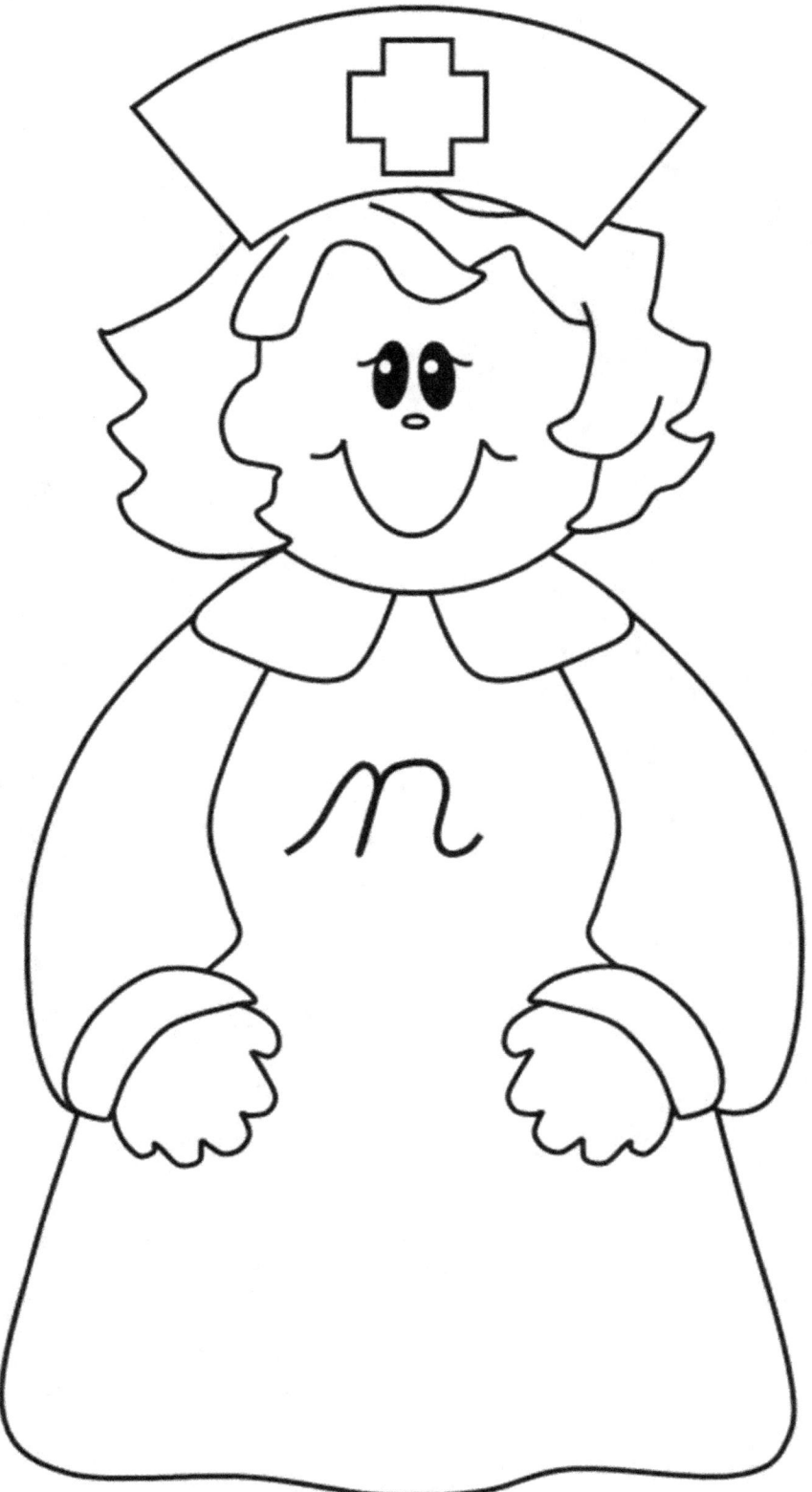

Trace the steps for making the letter n on the following line.

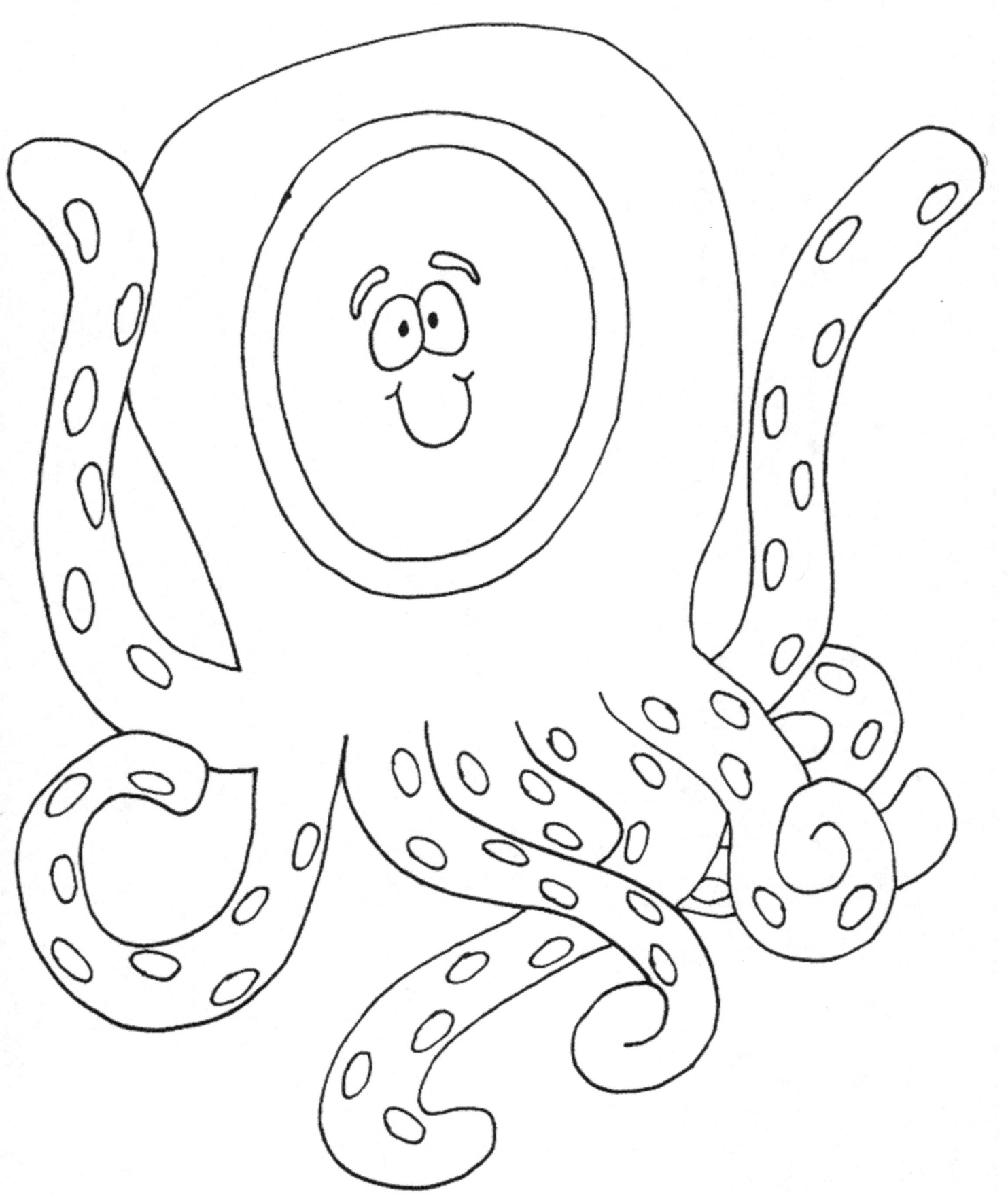

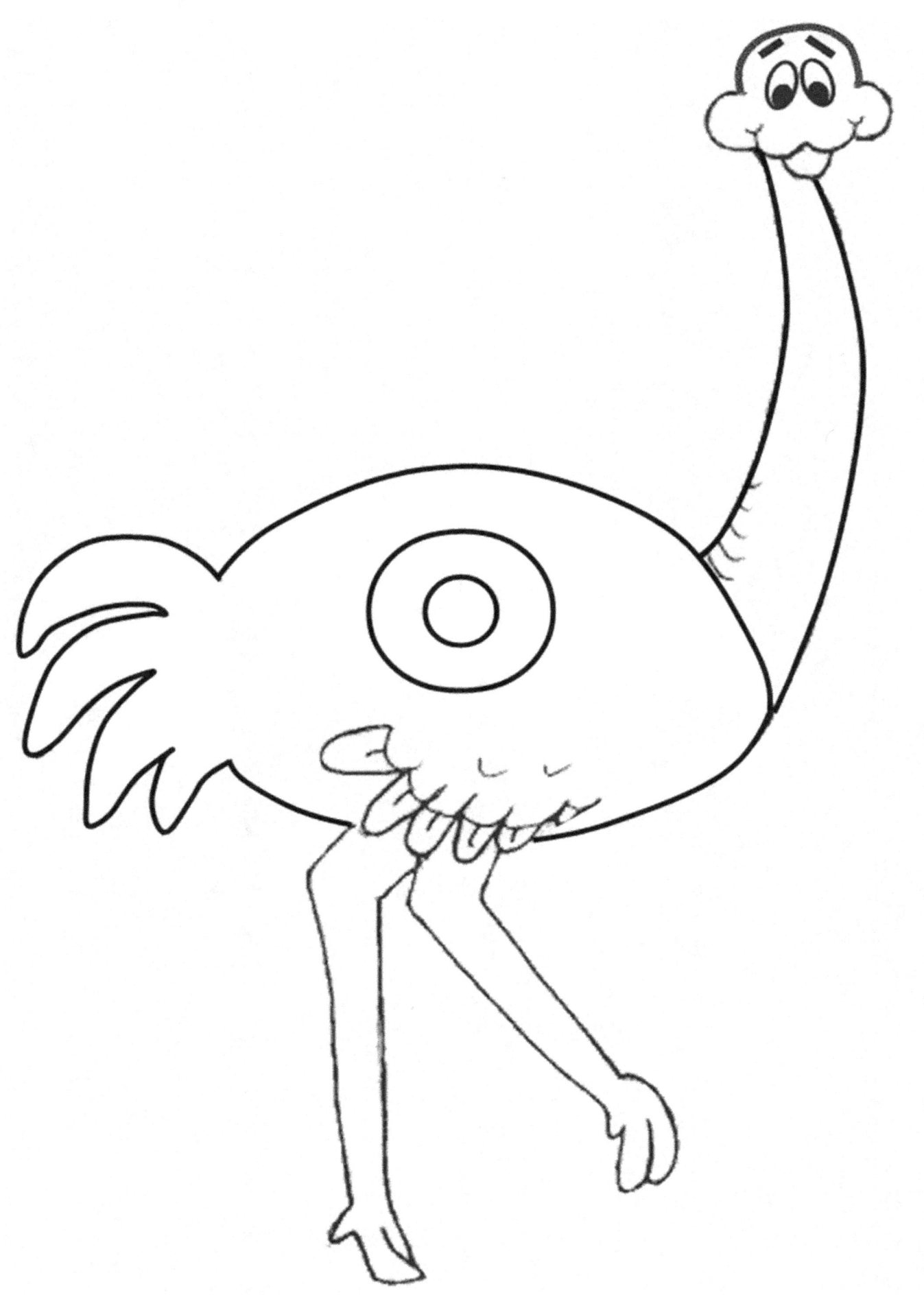

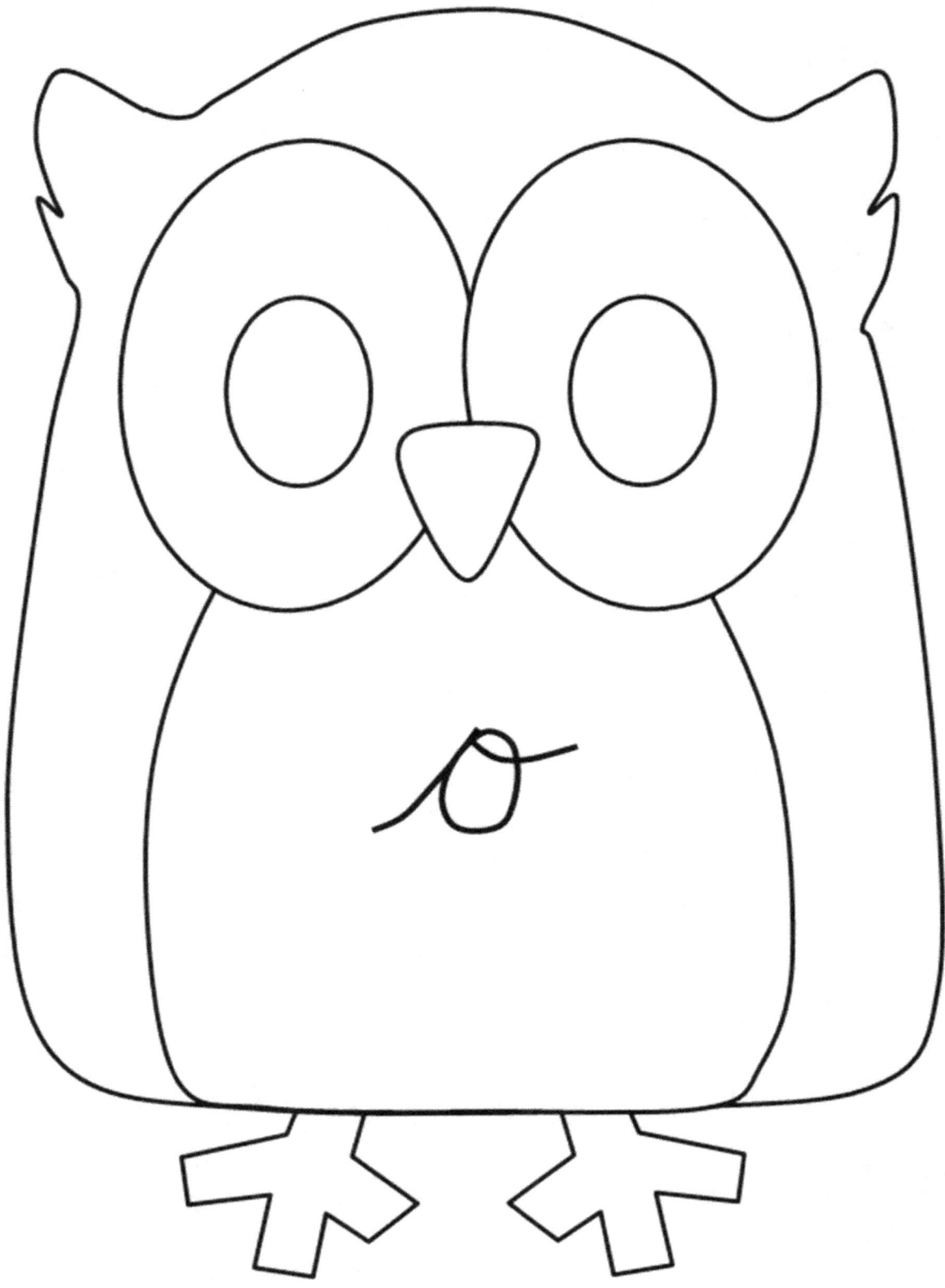

Trace the steps for making the letter o on the following line.

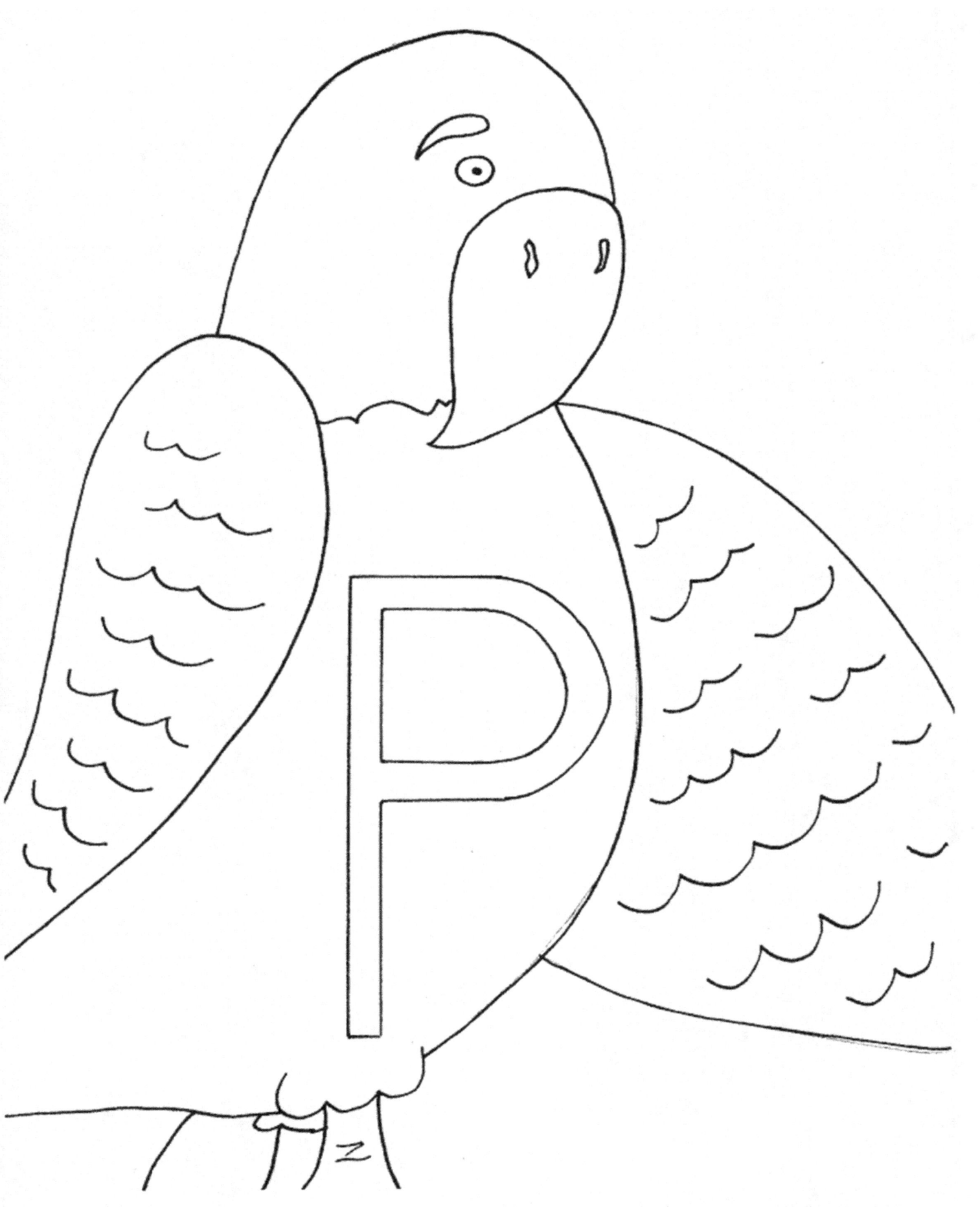

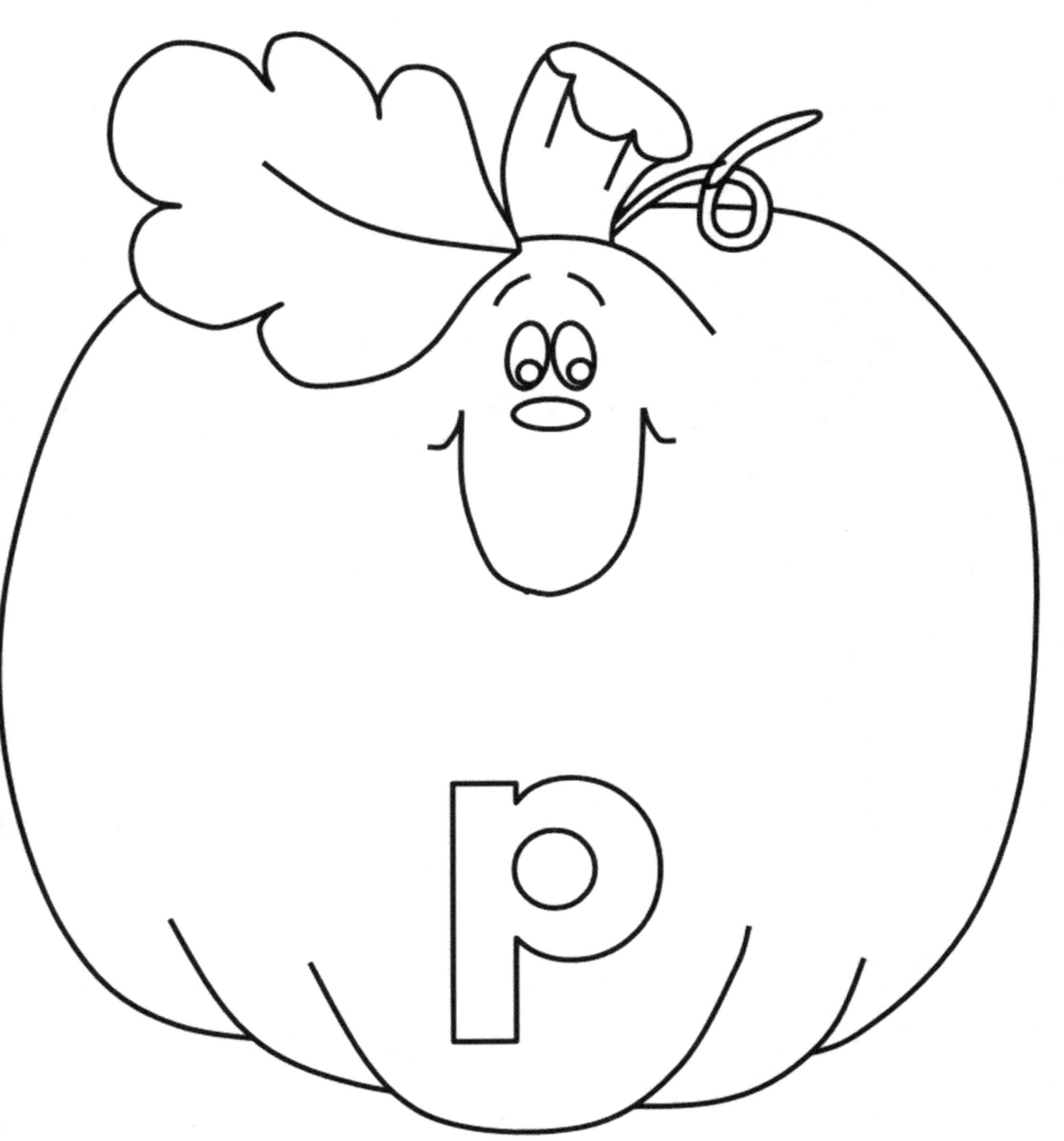

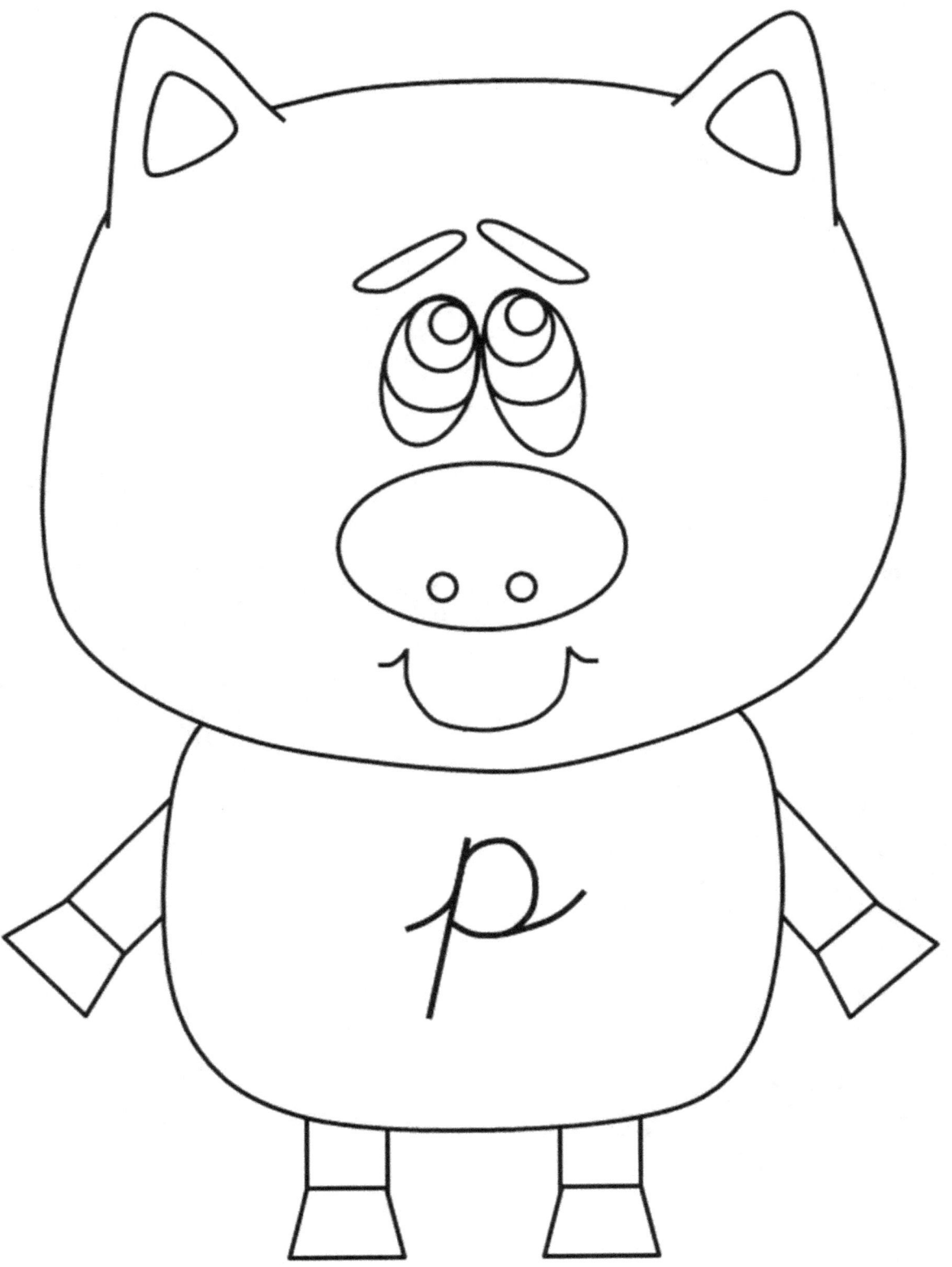

Trace the steps for making the letter p on the following line.

$\mathcal{P}$ $\mathcal{P}$ $\mathcal{P}$ $\mathcal{P}$ $\mathcal{P}$ $\mathcal{P}$ $\mathcal{PP}$

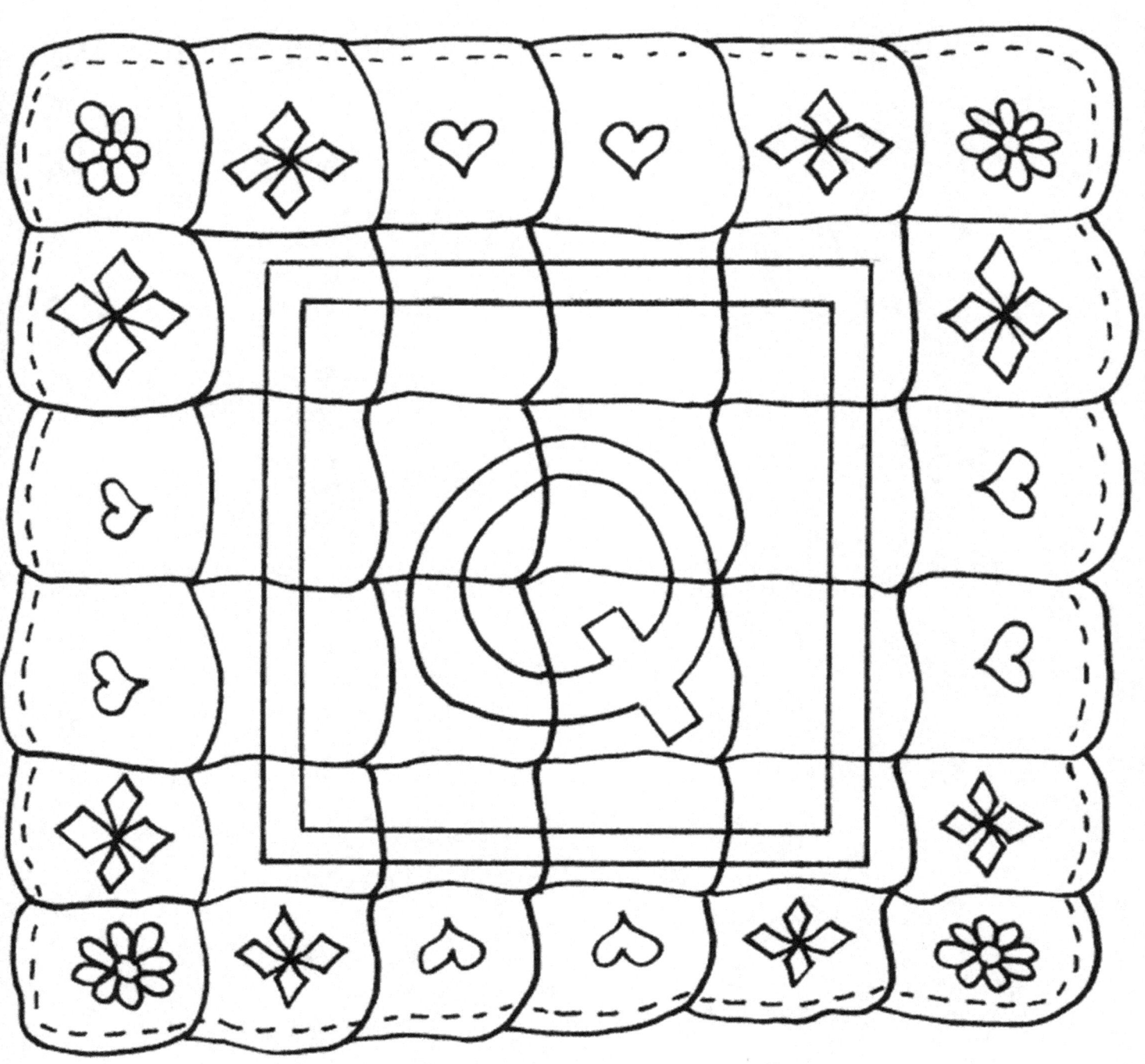

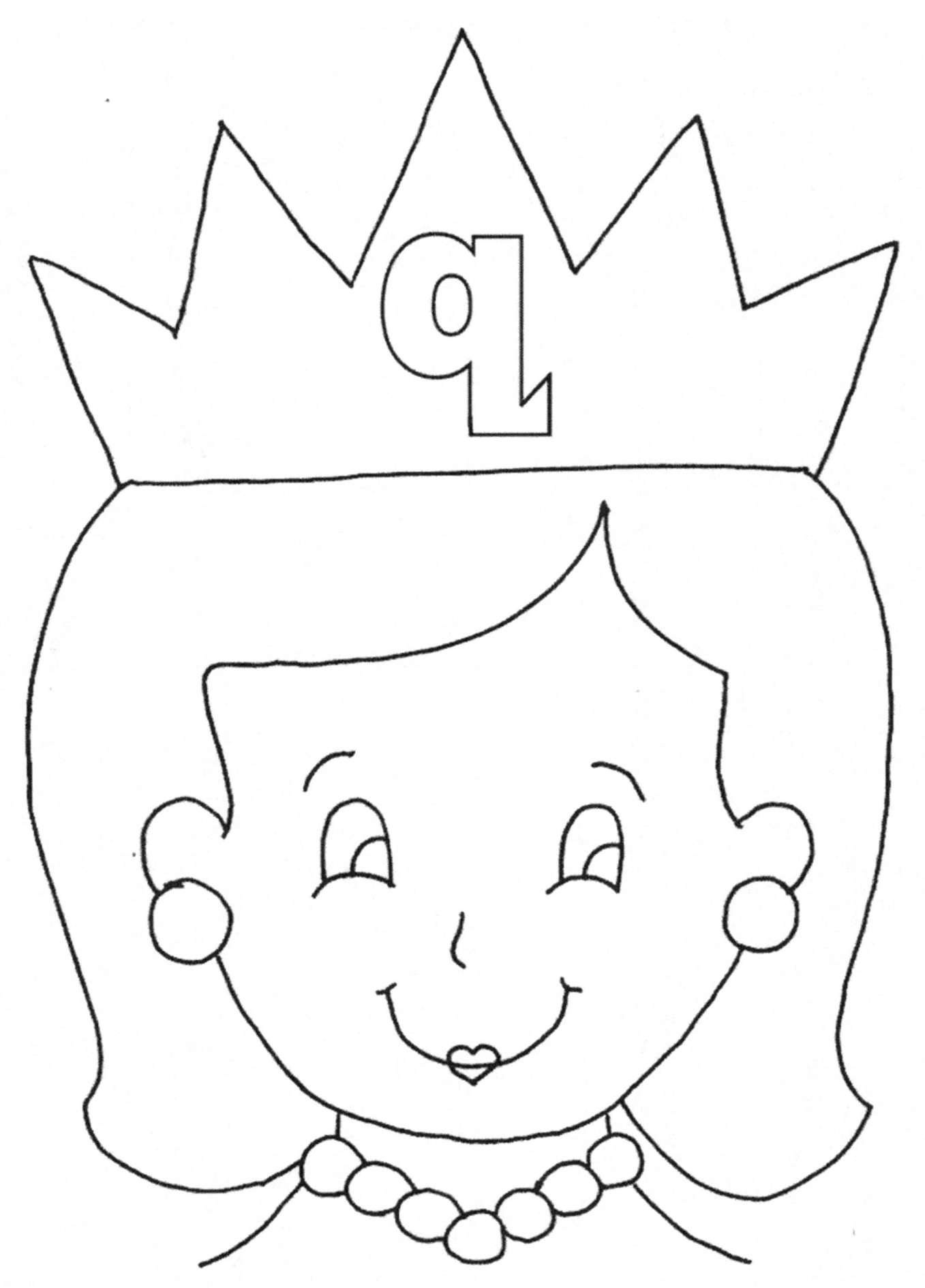

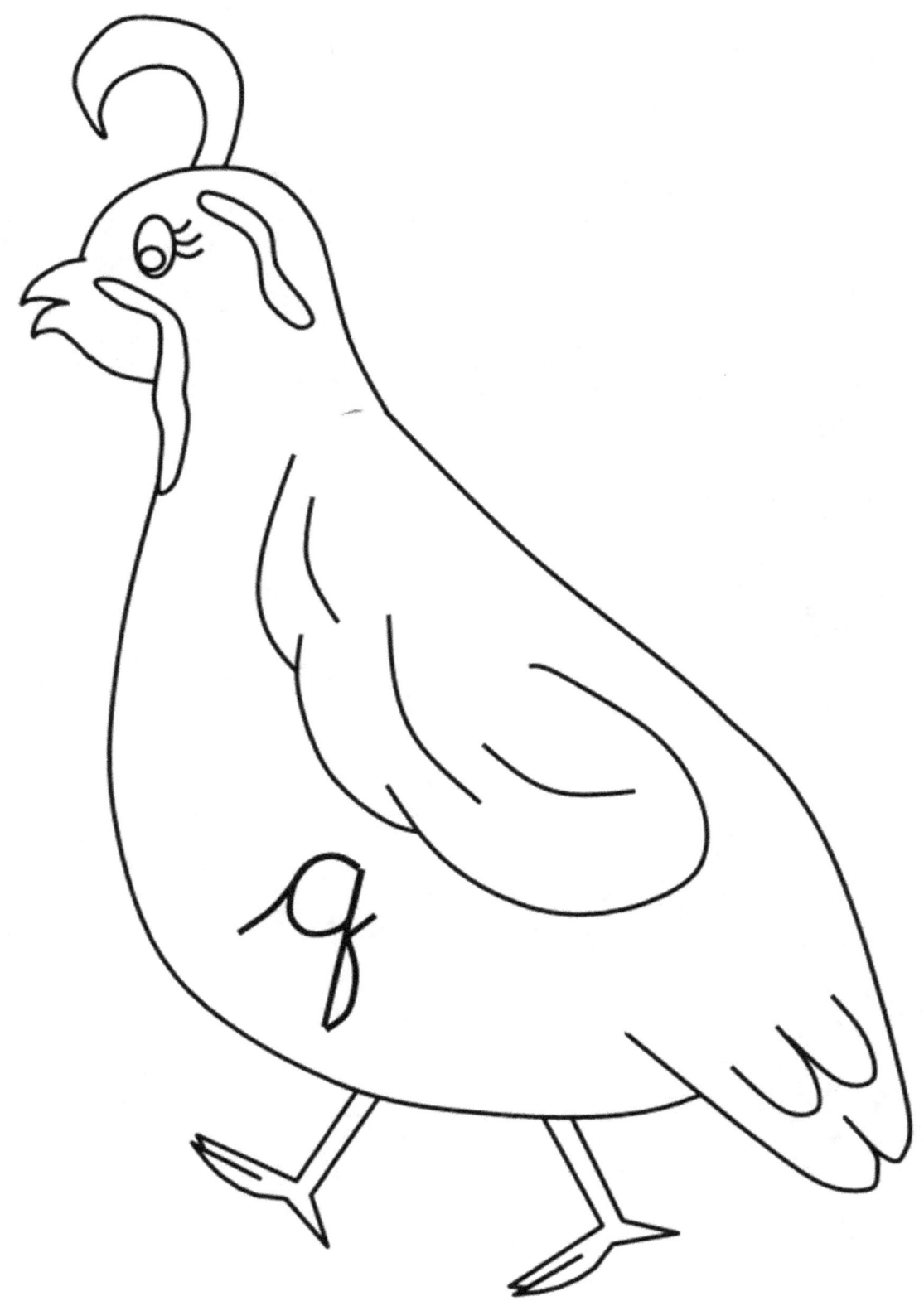

Trace the steps for making the letter q on the following line.

$\int \quad \int \quad \sigma \quad q \quad q \quad q \quad q$

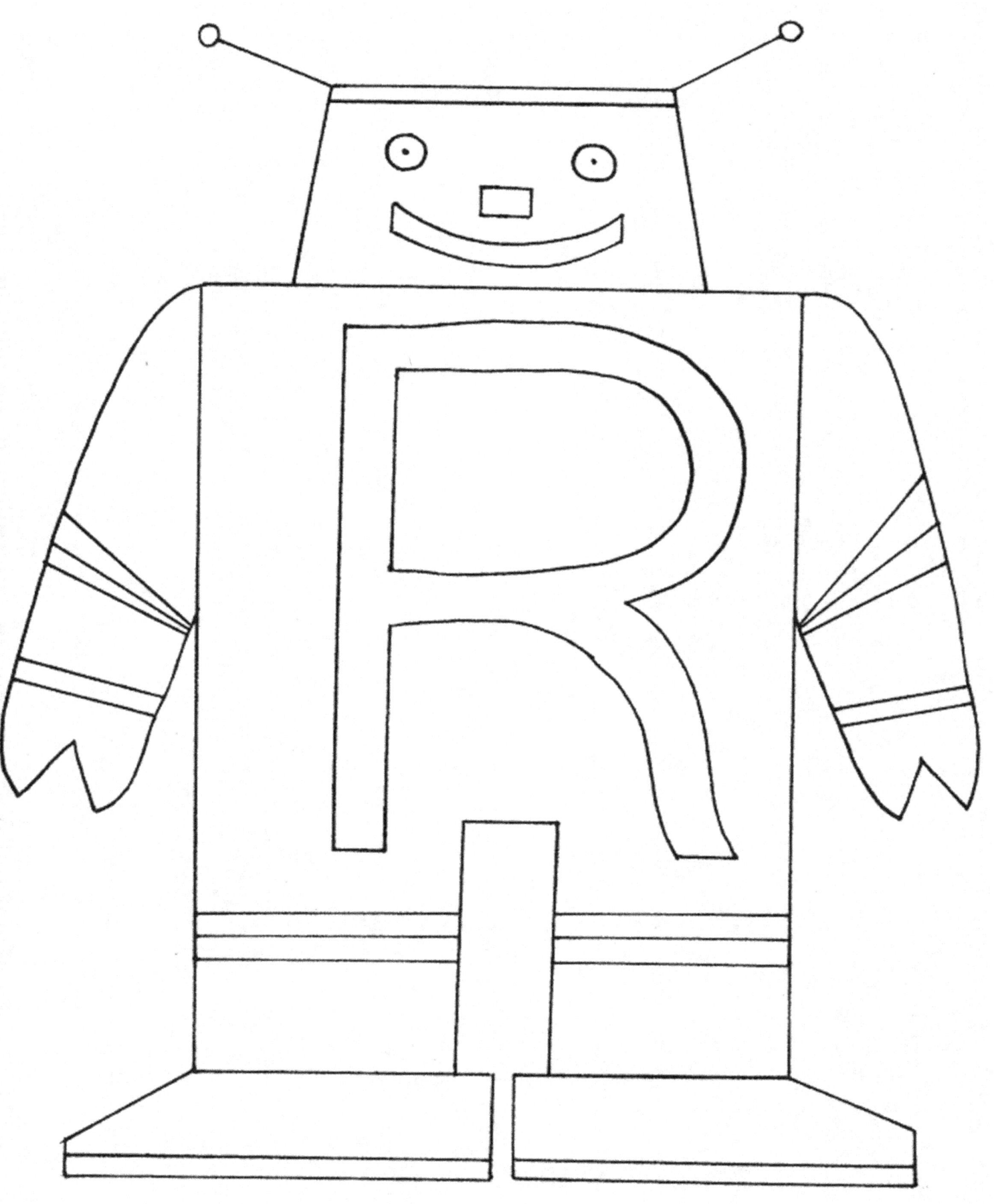

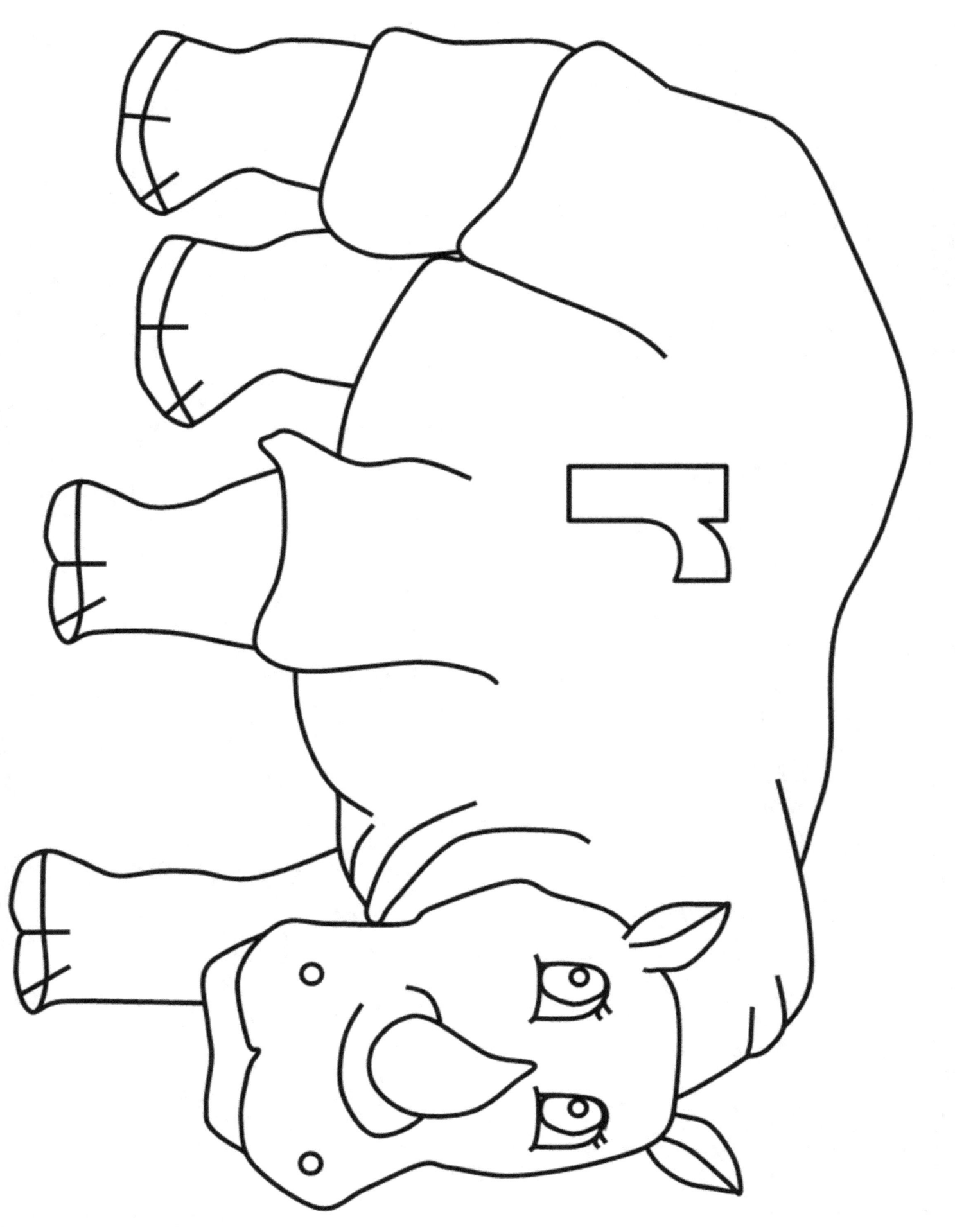

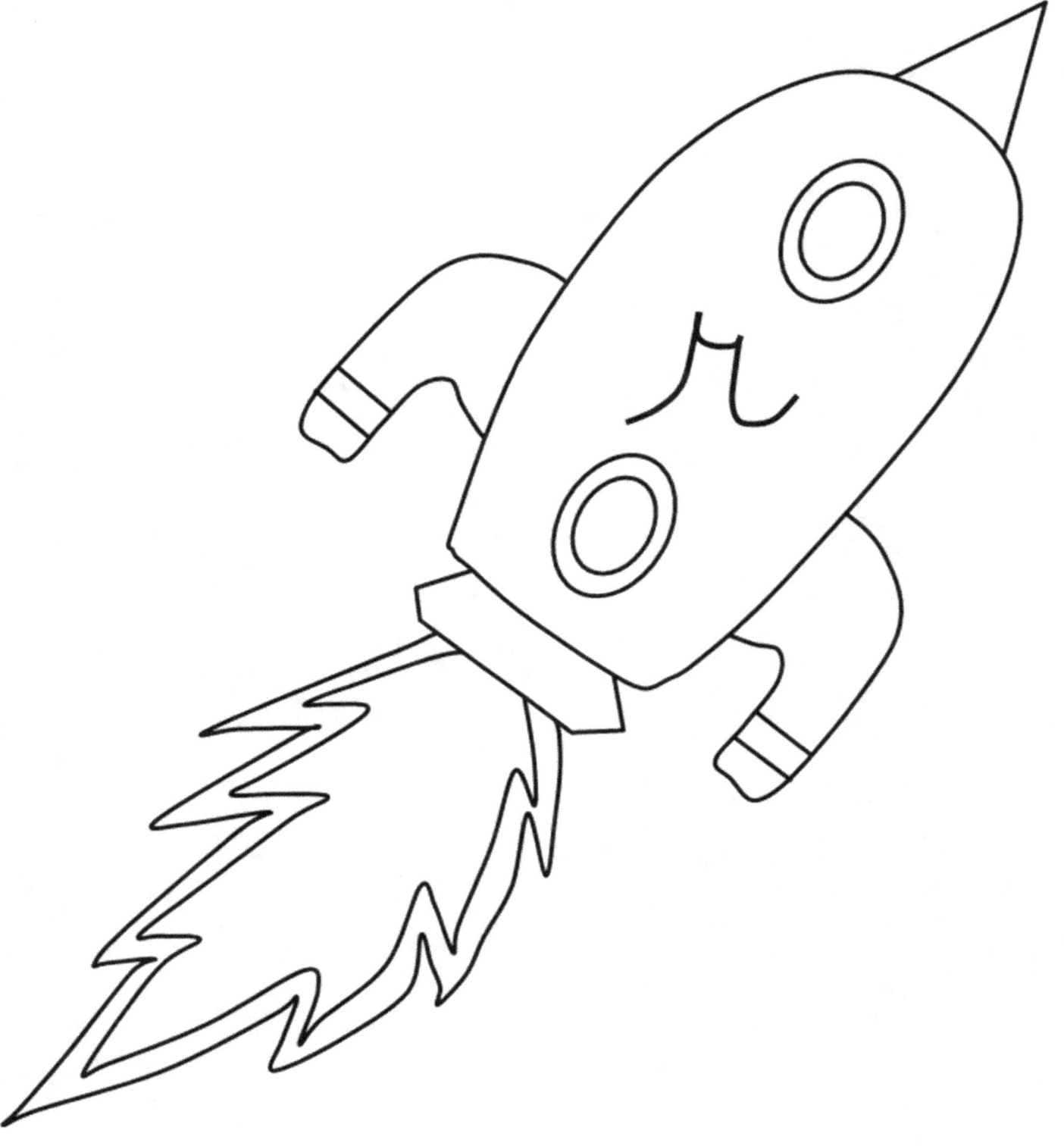

Trace the steps for making the letter r on the following line.

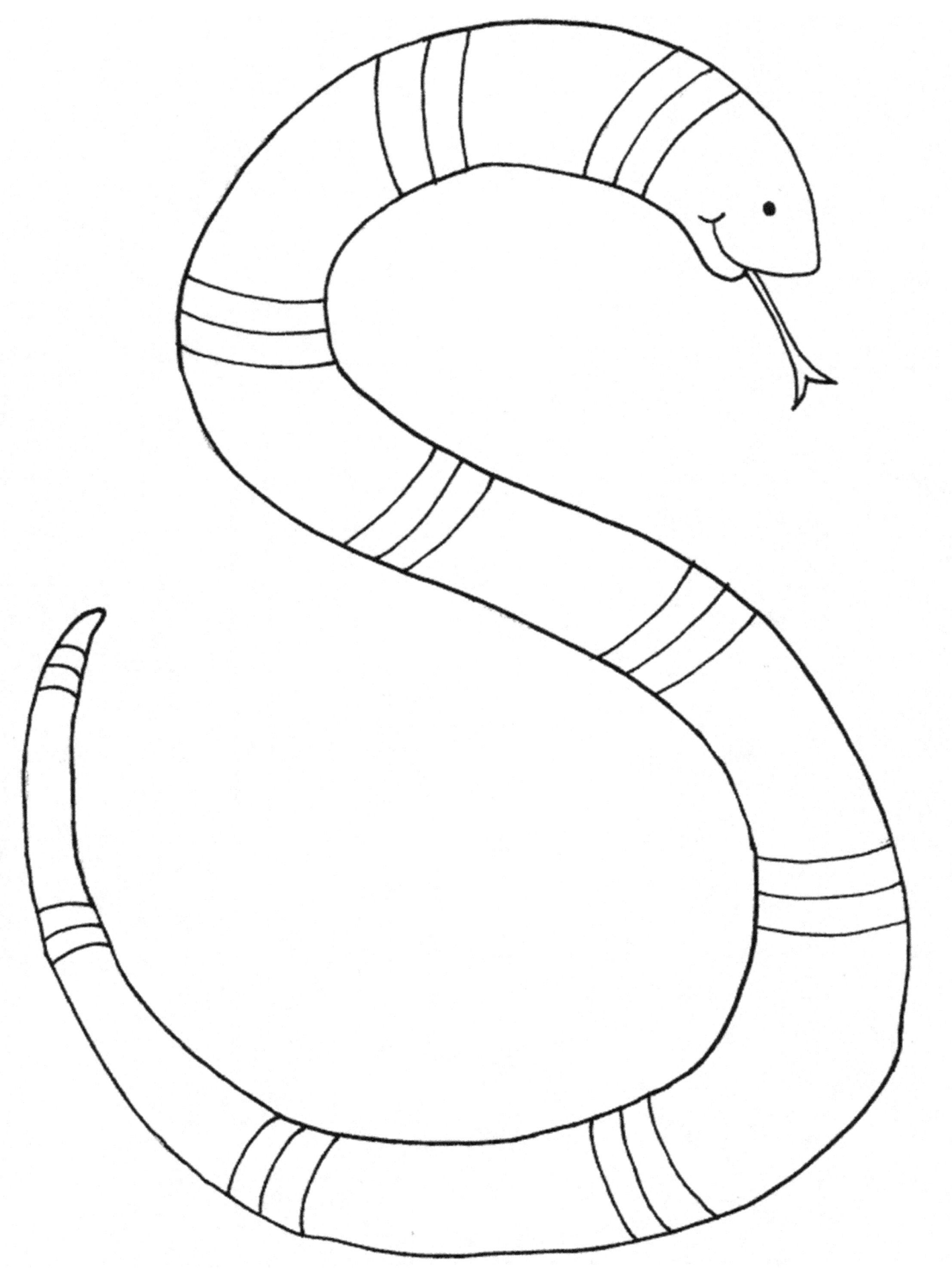

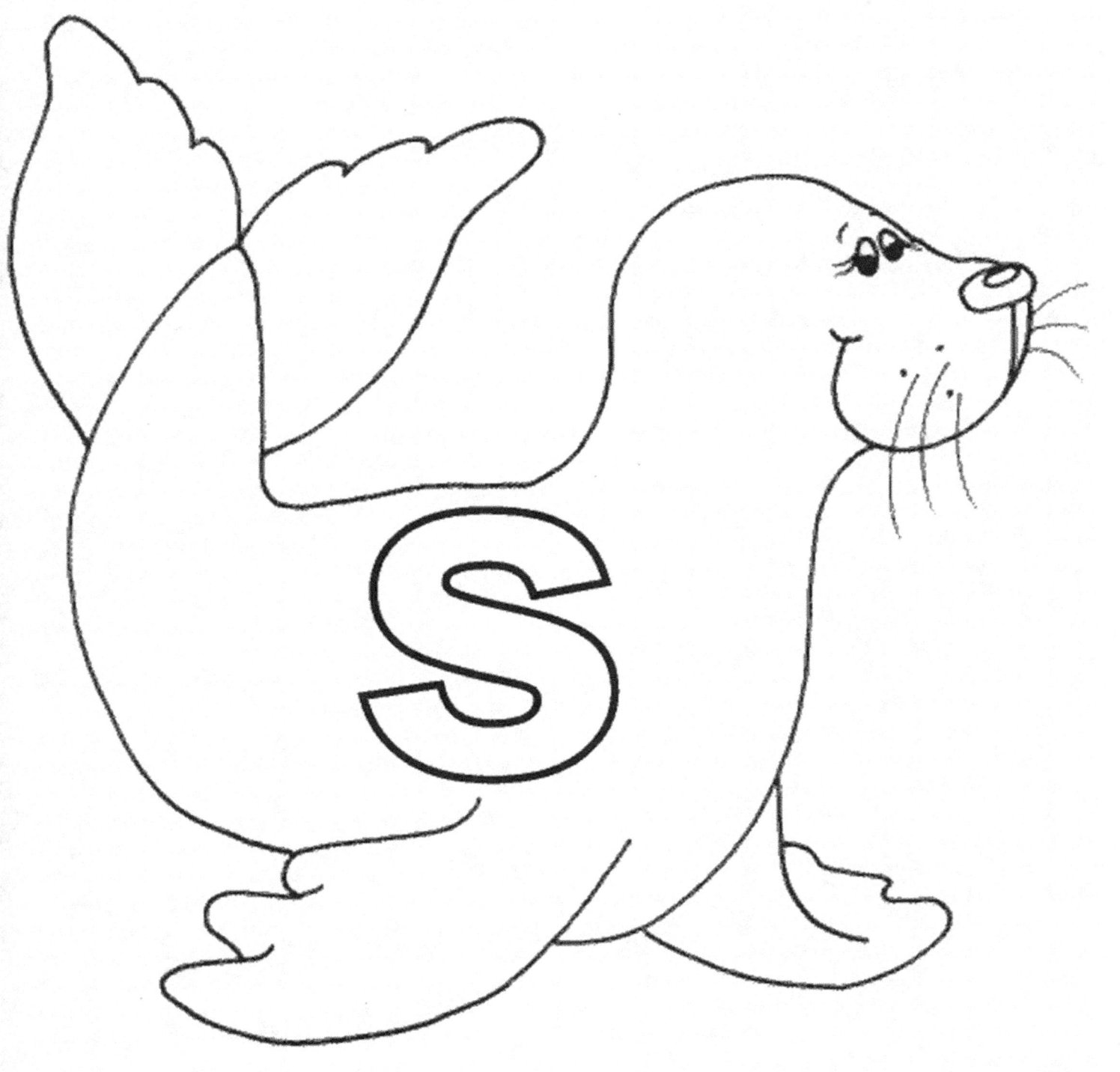

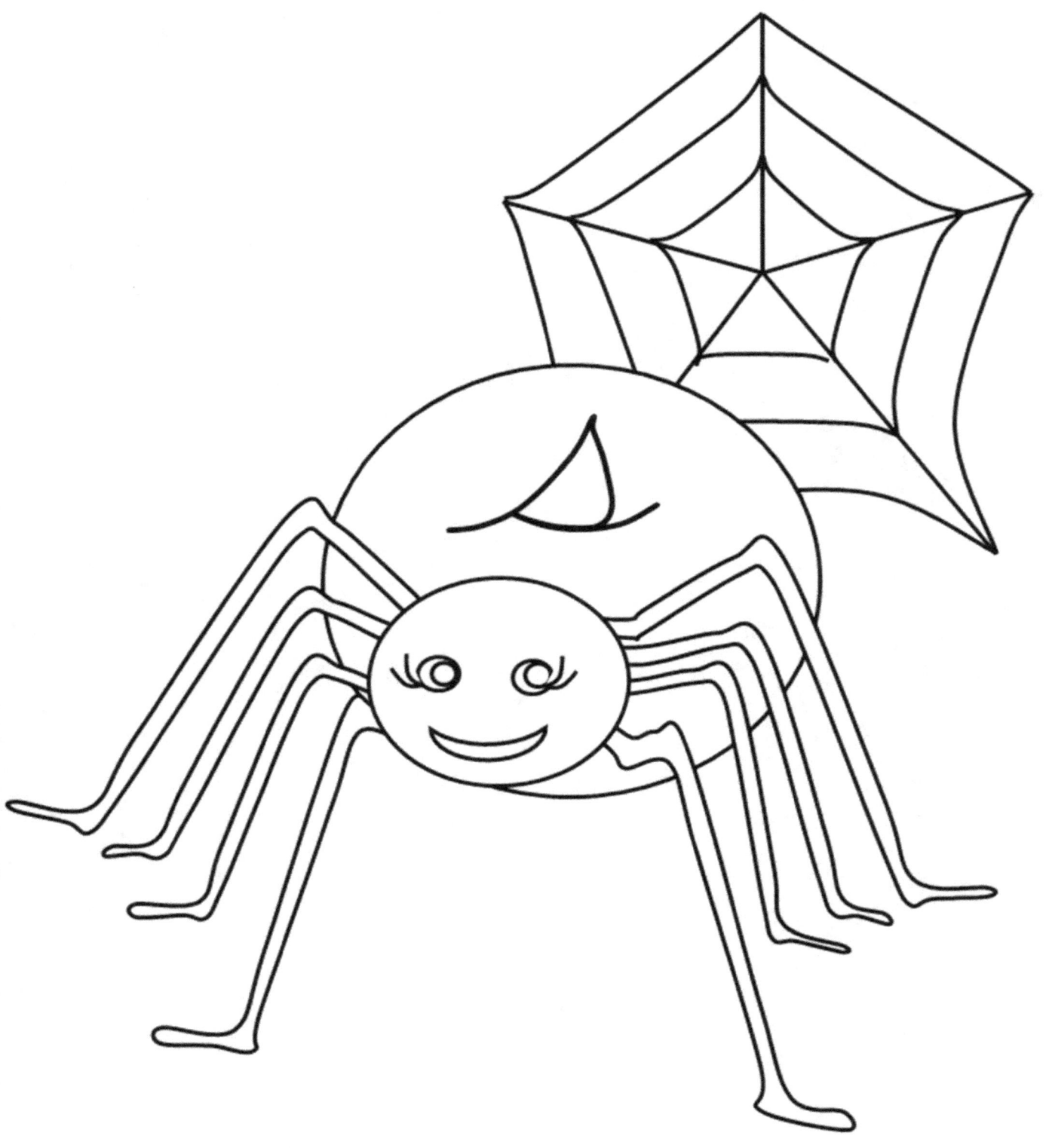

Trace the steps for making the letter s on the following line.

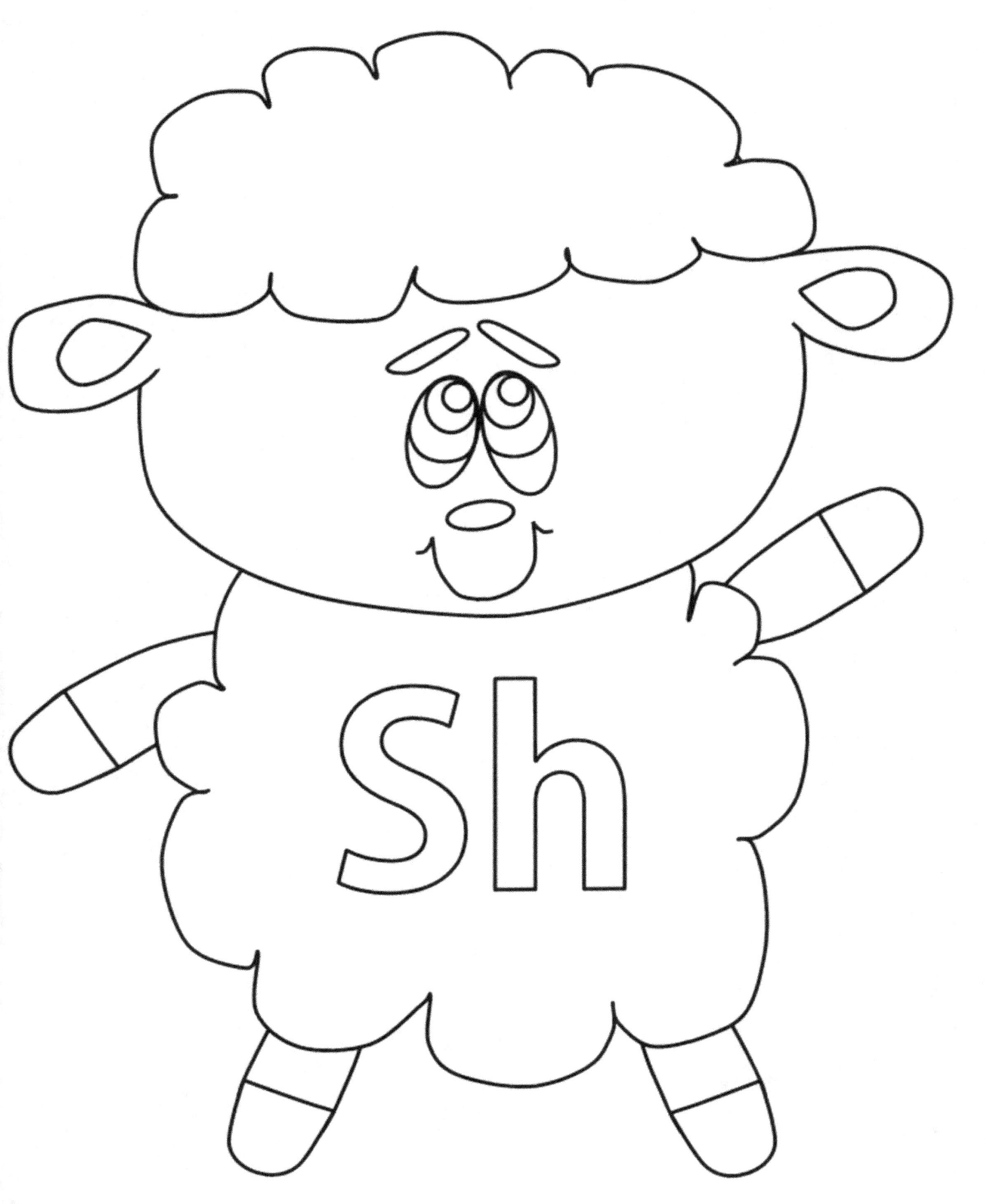

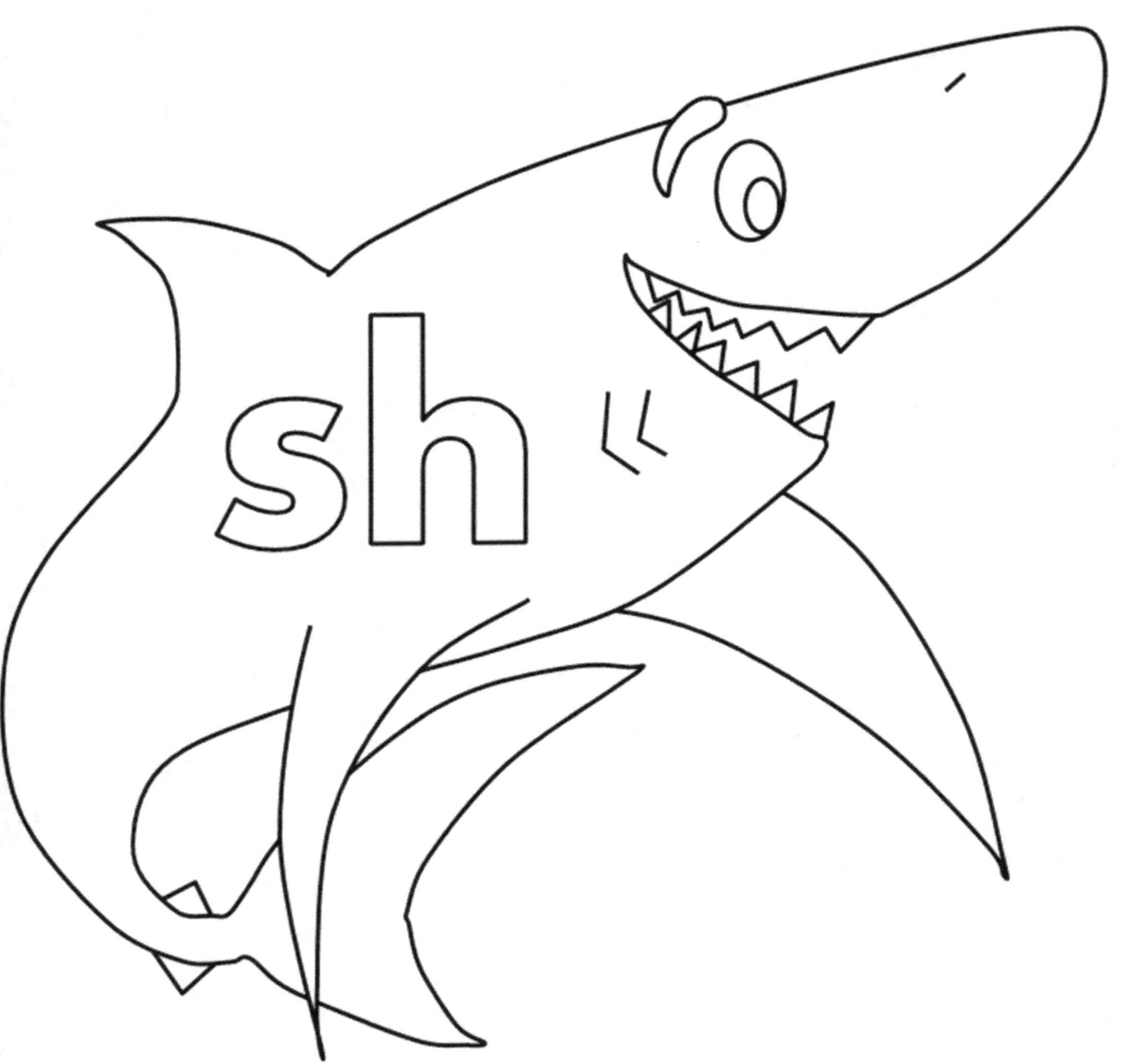

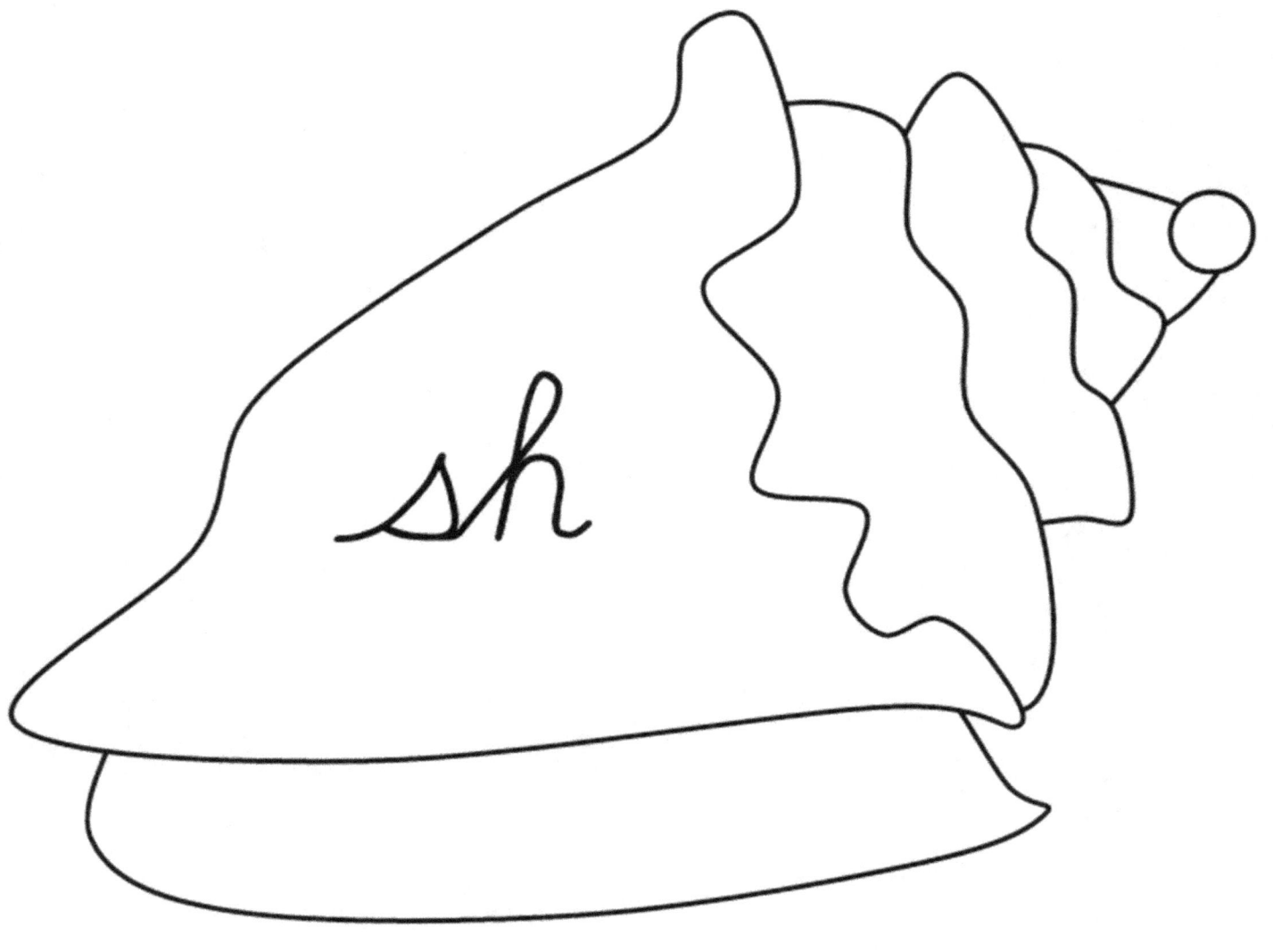

Trace the steps for making the letter sh on the following line.

s h sh sh sh

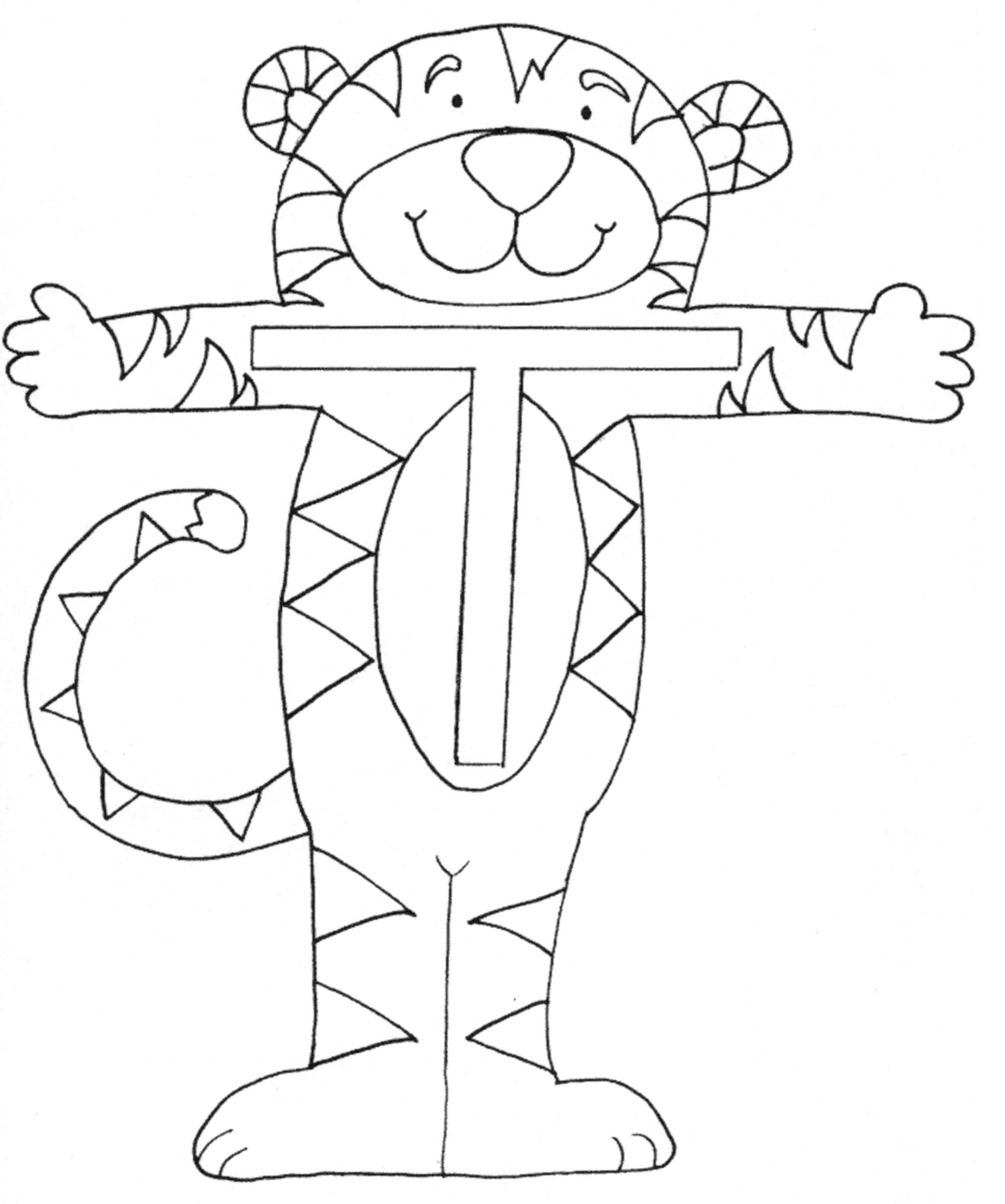

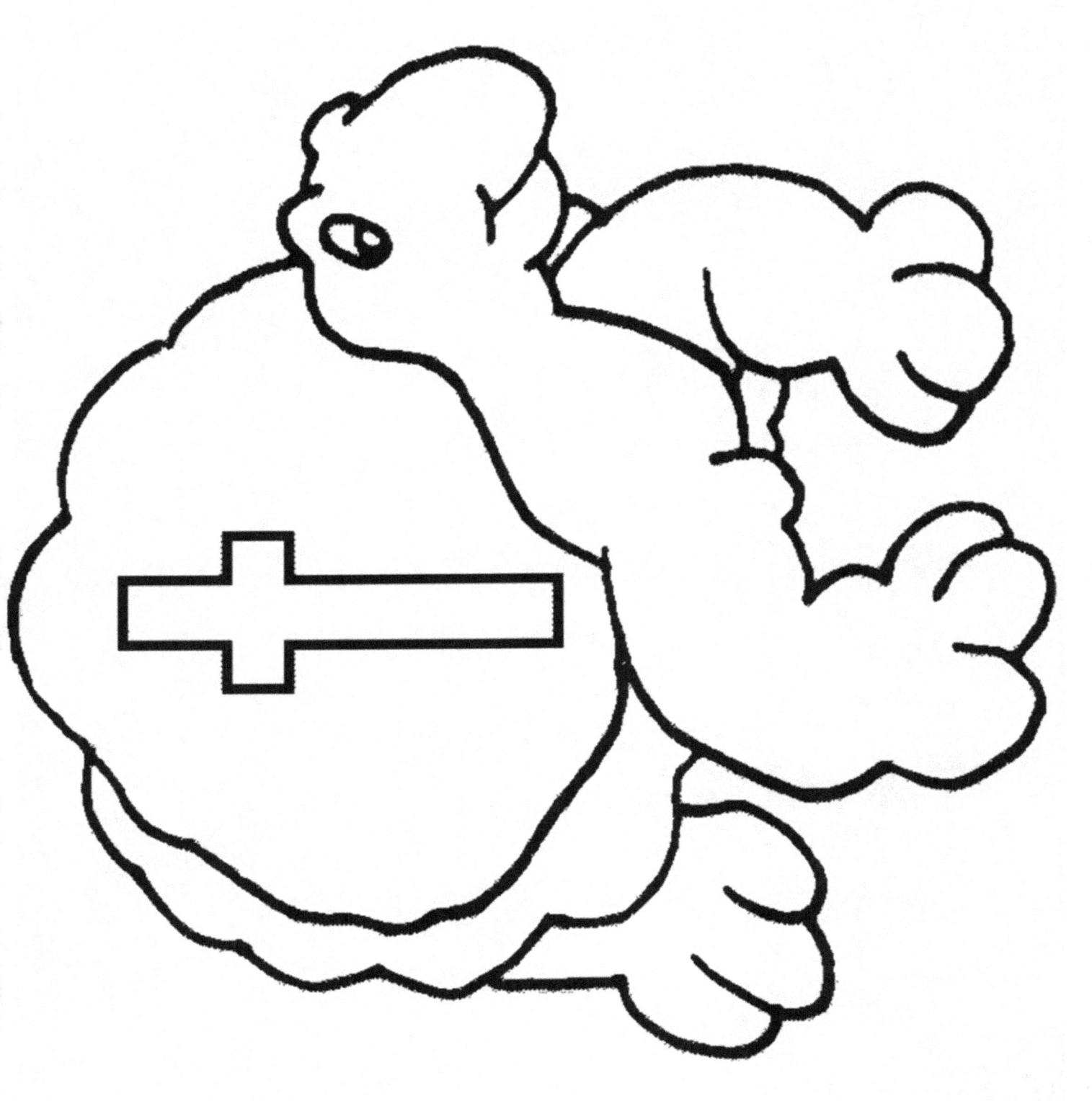

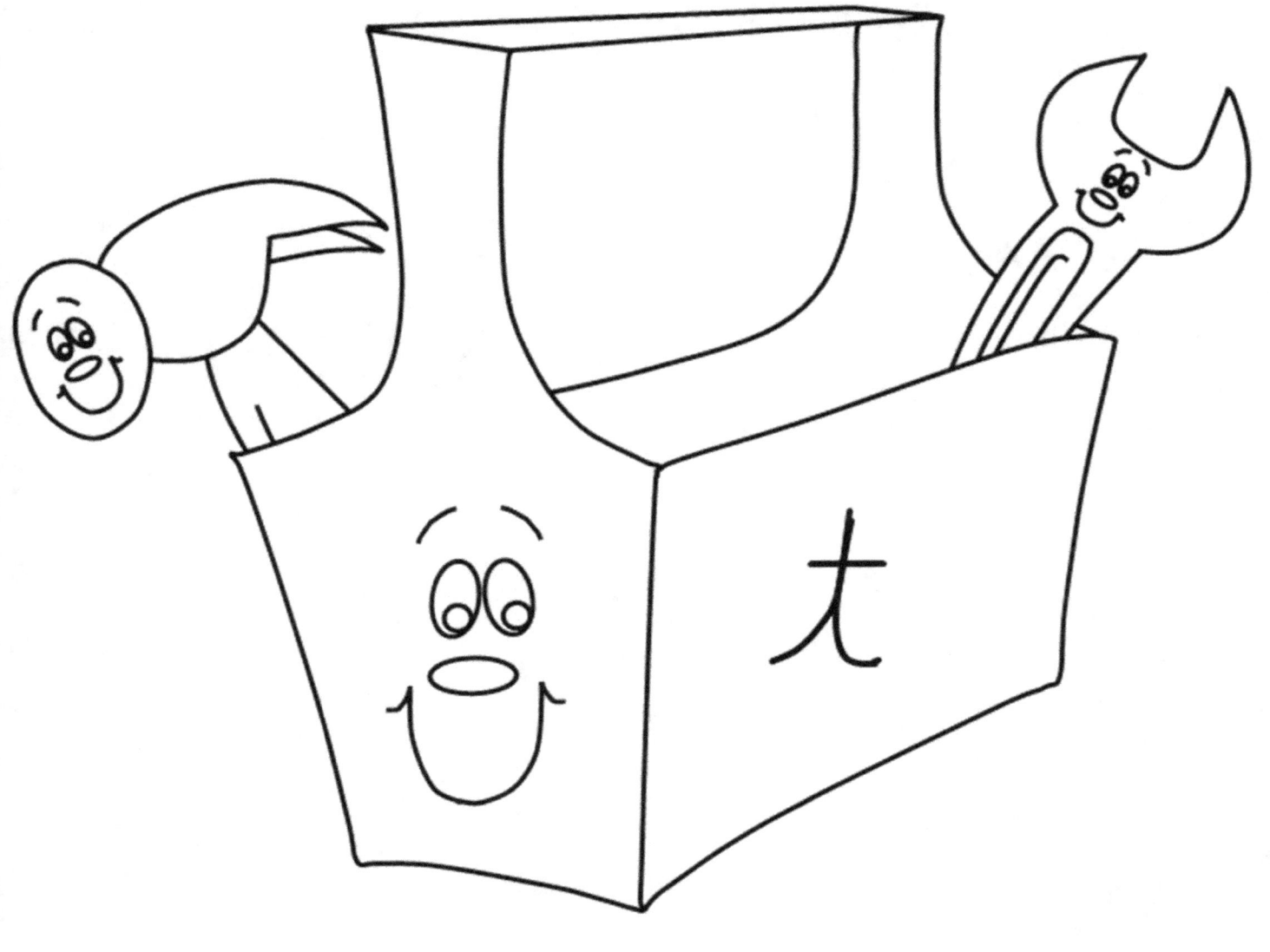

Trace the steps for making the letter t on the following line.

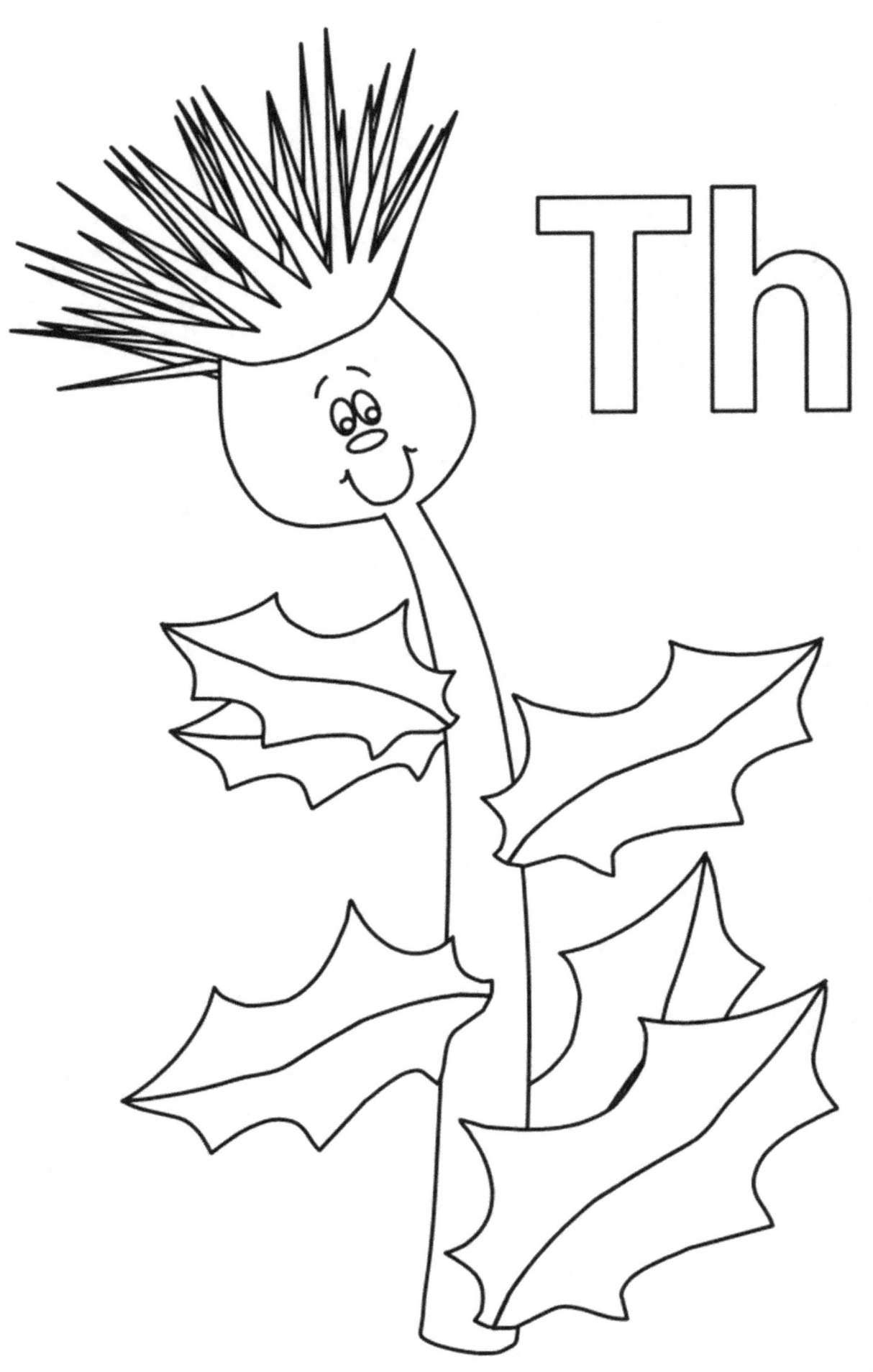

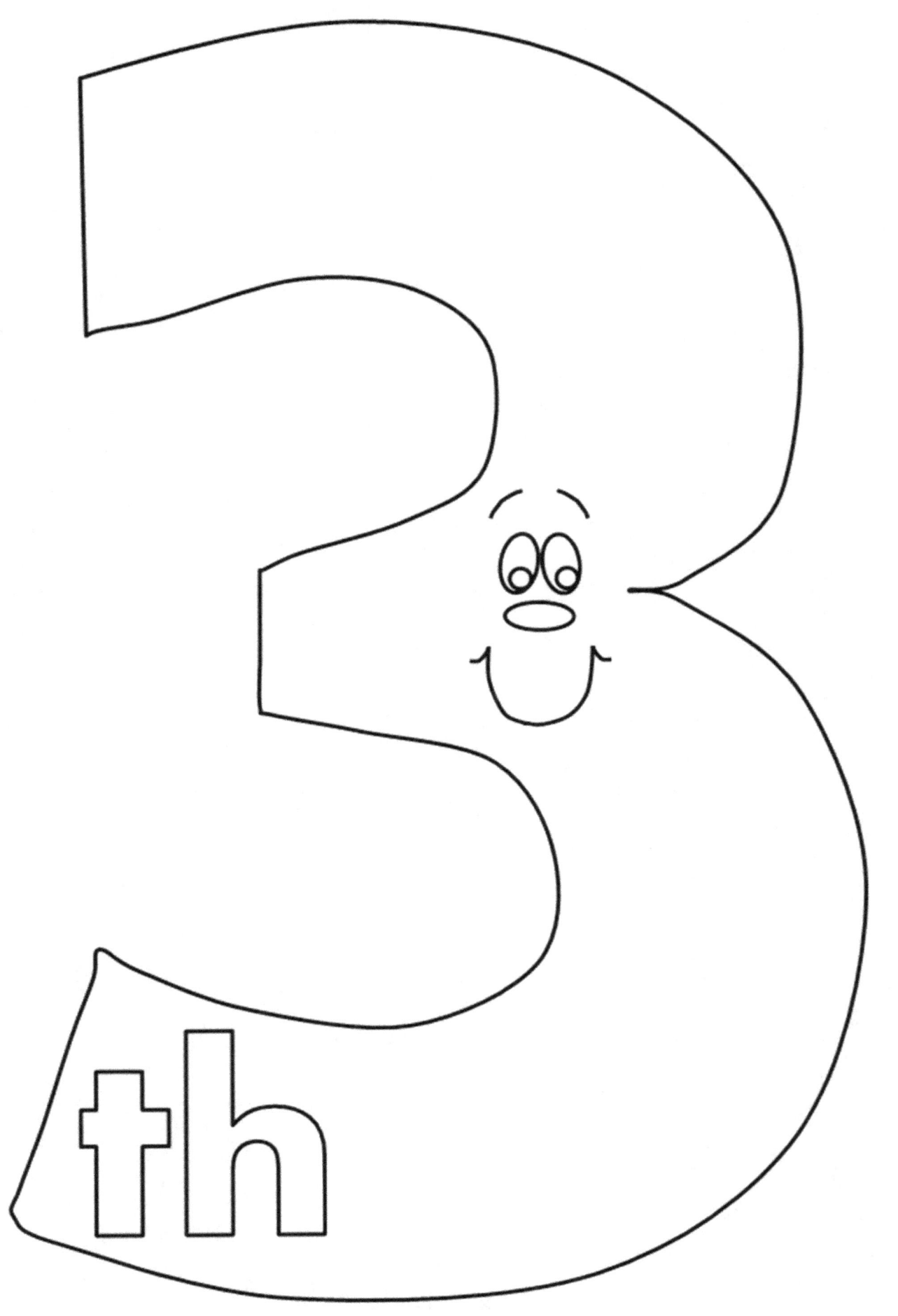

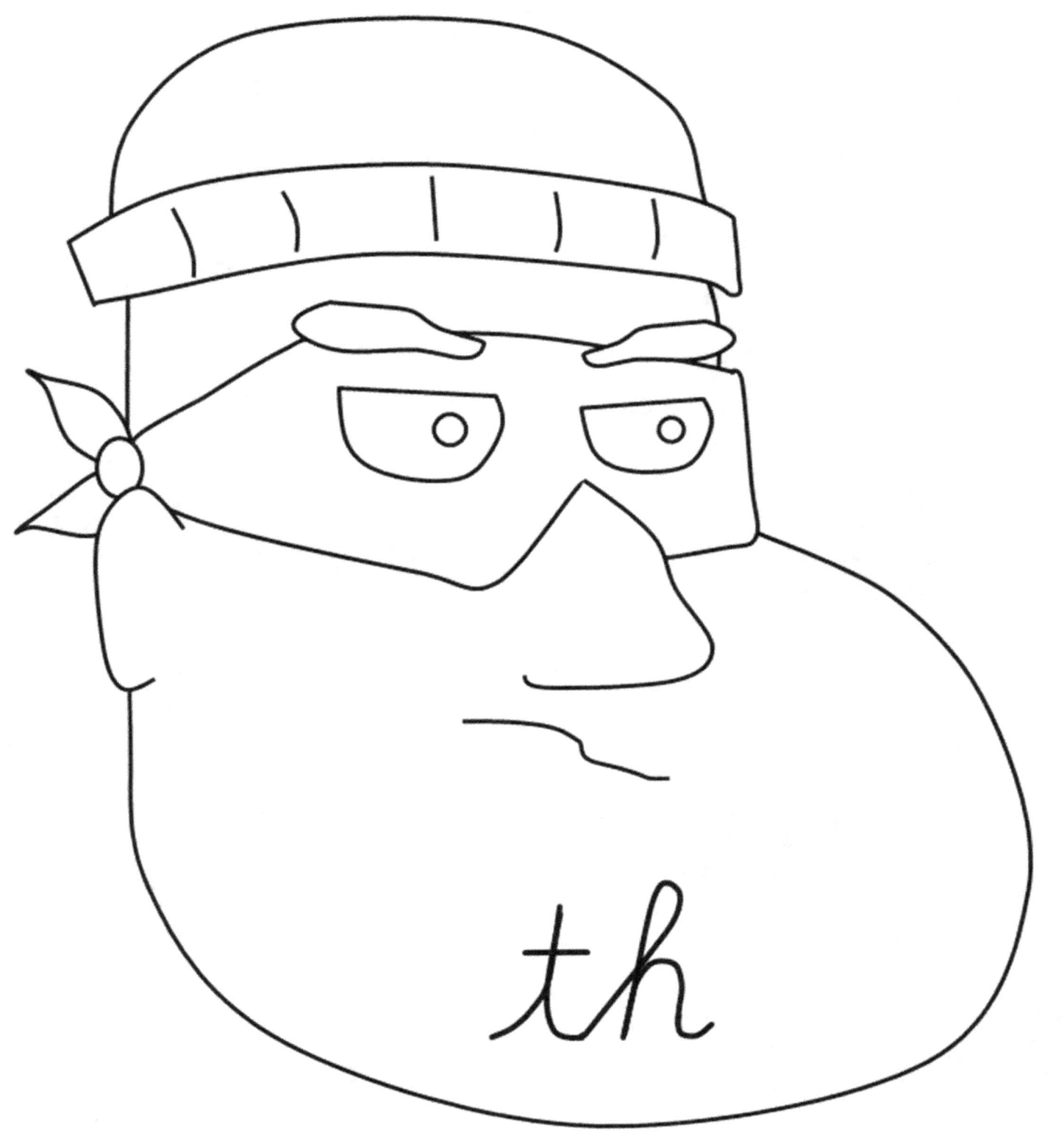

Trace the steps for making the letter th on the following line.

_t_ _h_ _th_ _th_ _th_ _th_

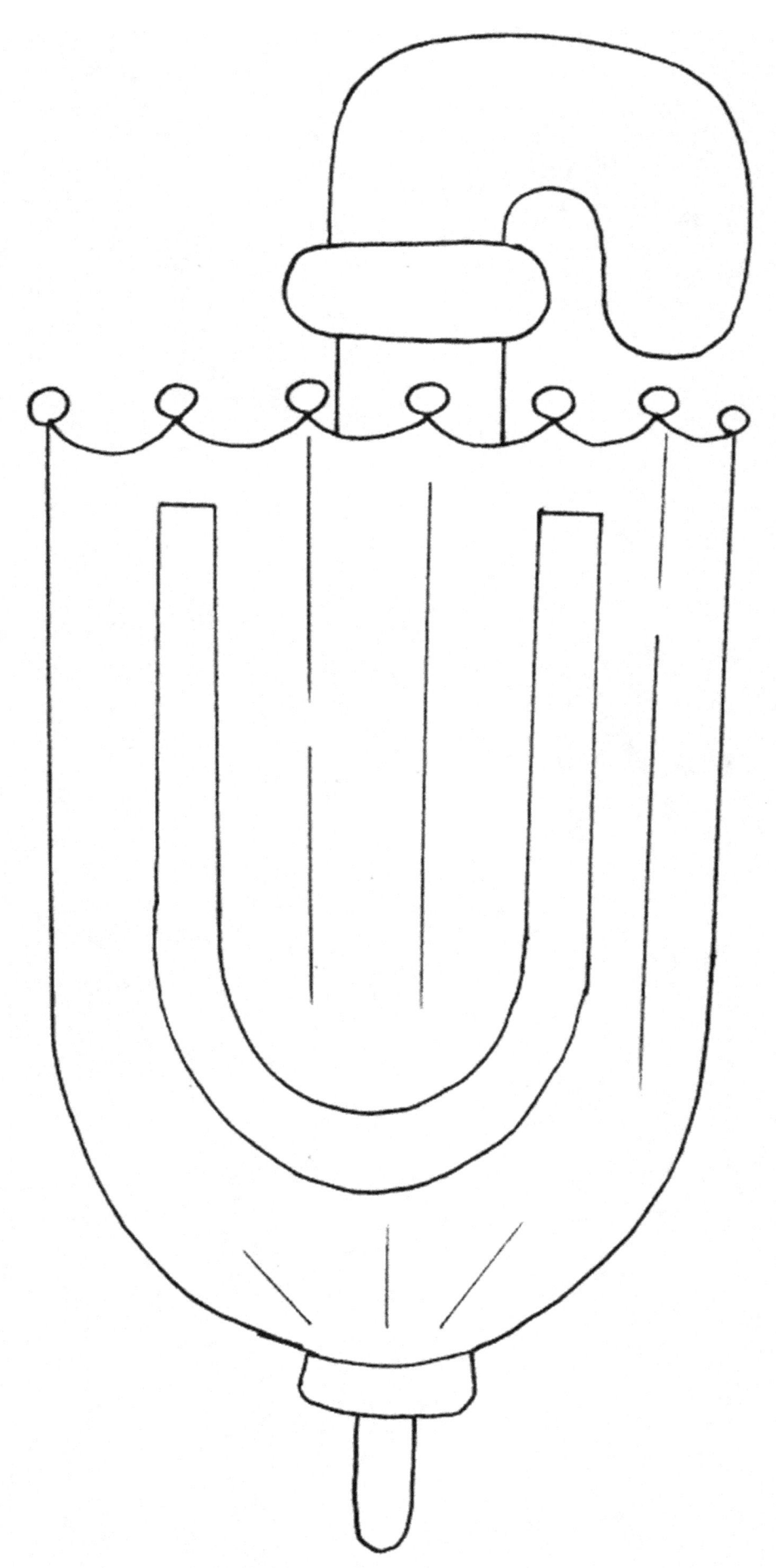

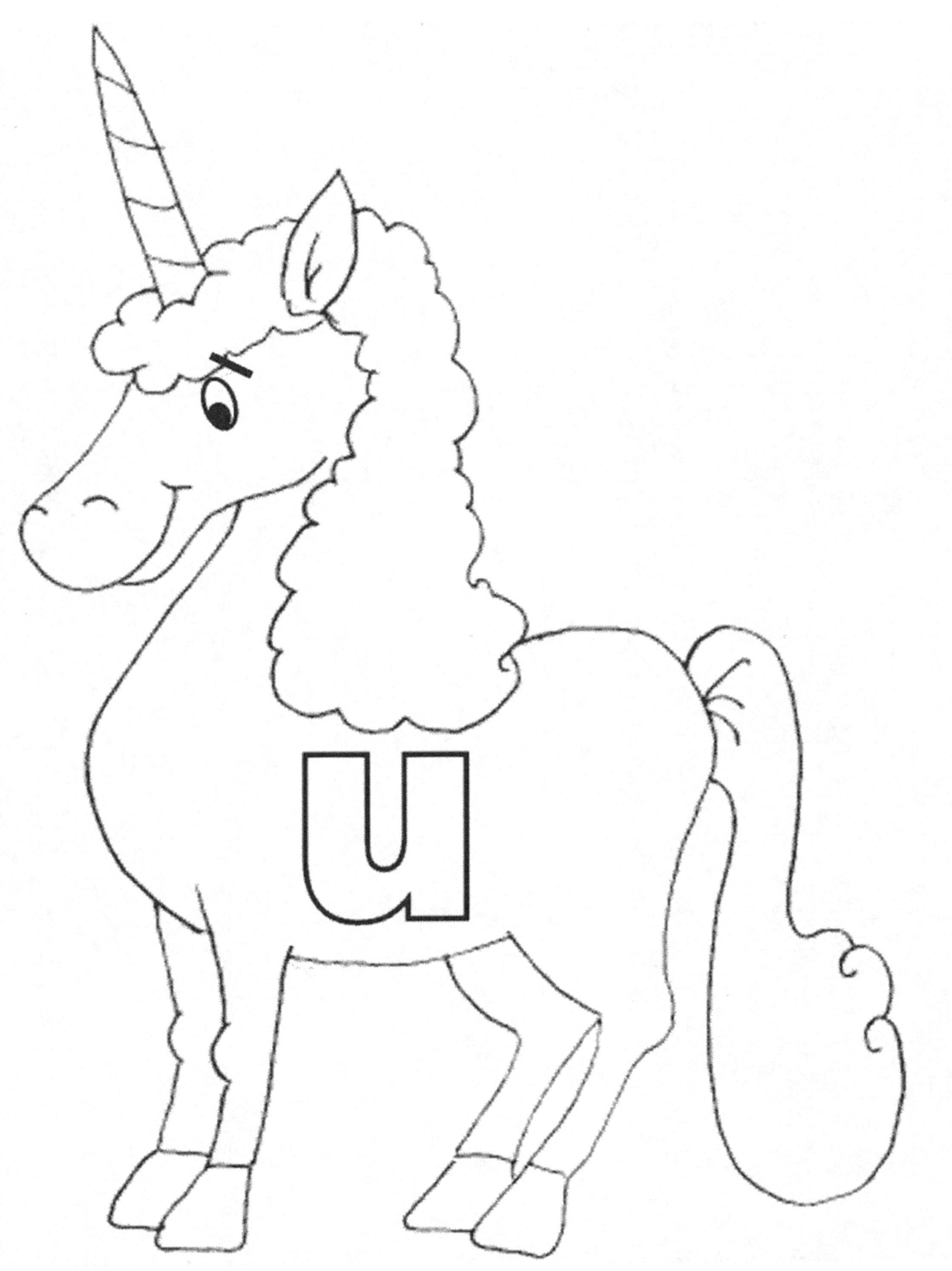

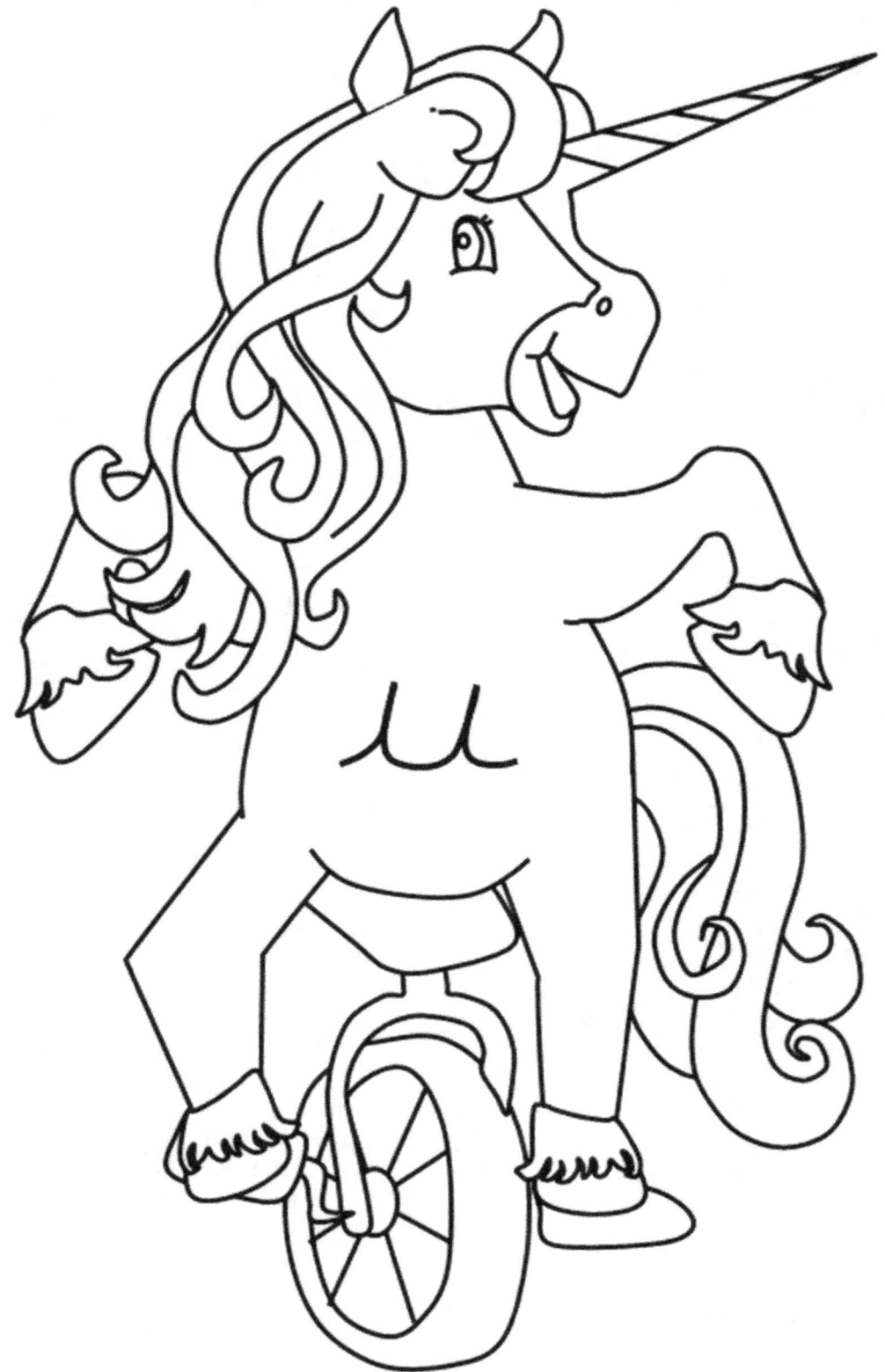

Trace the steps for making the letter u on the following line.

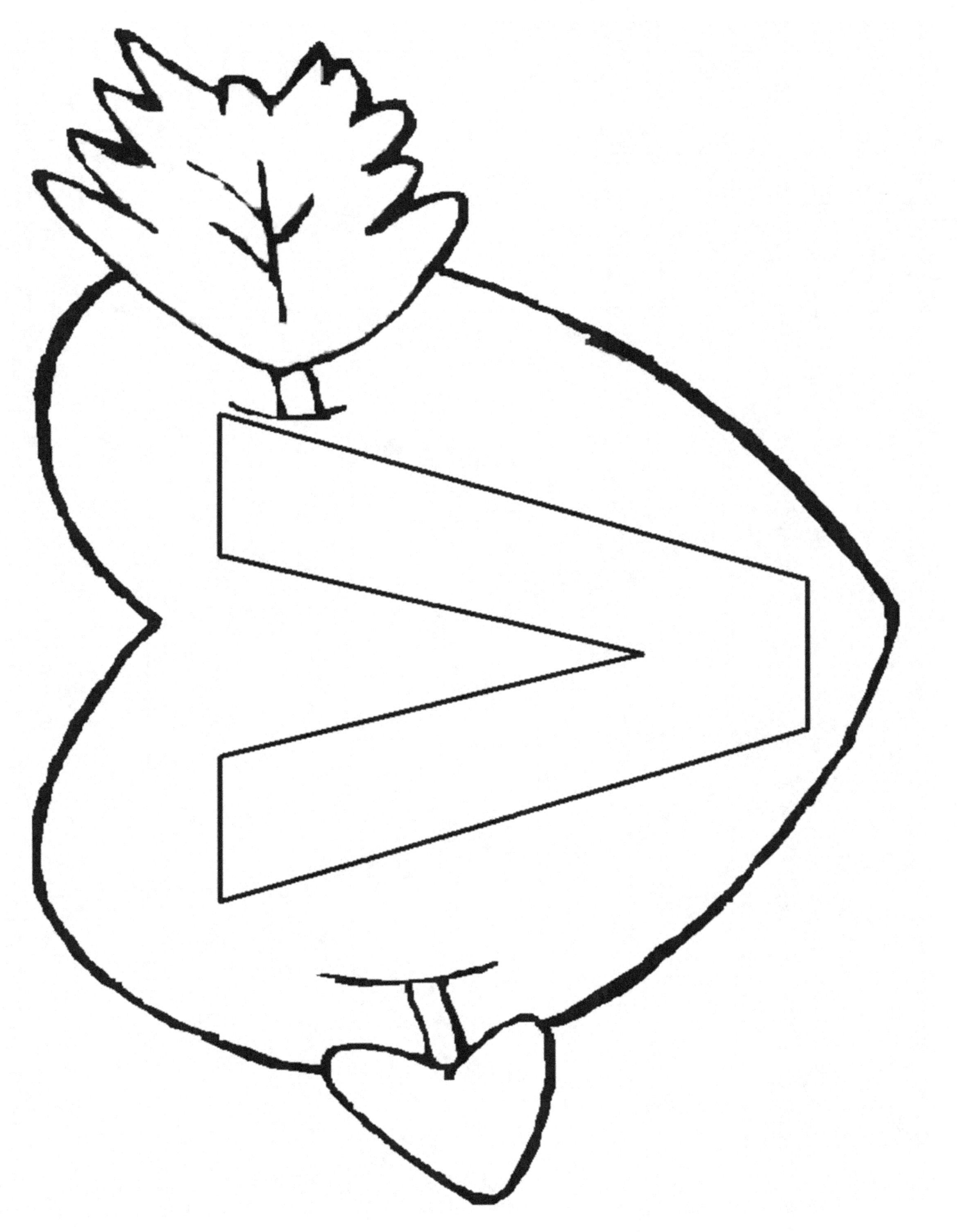

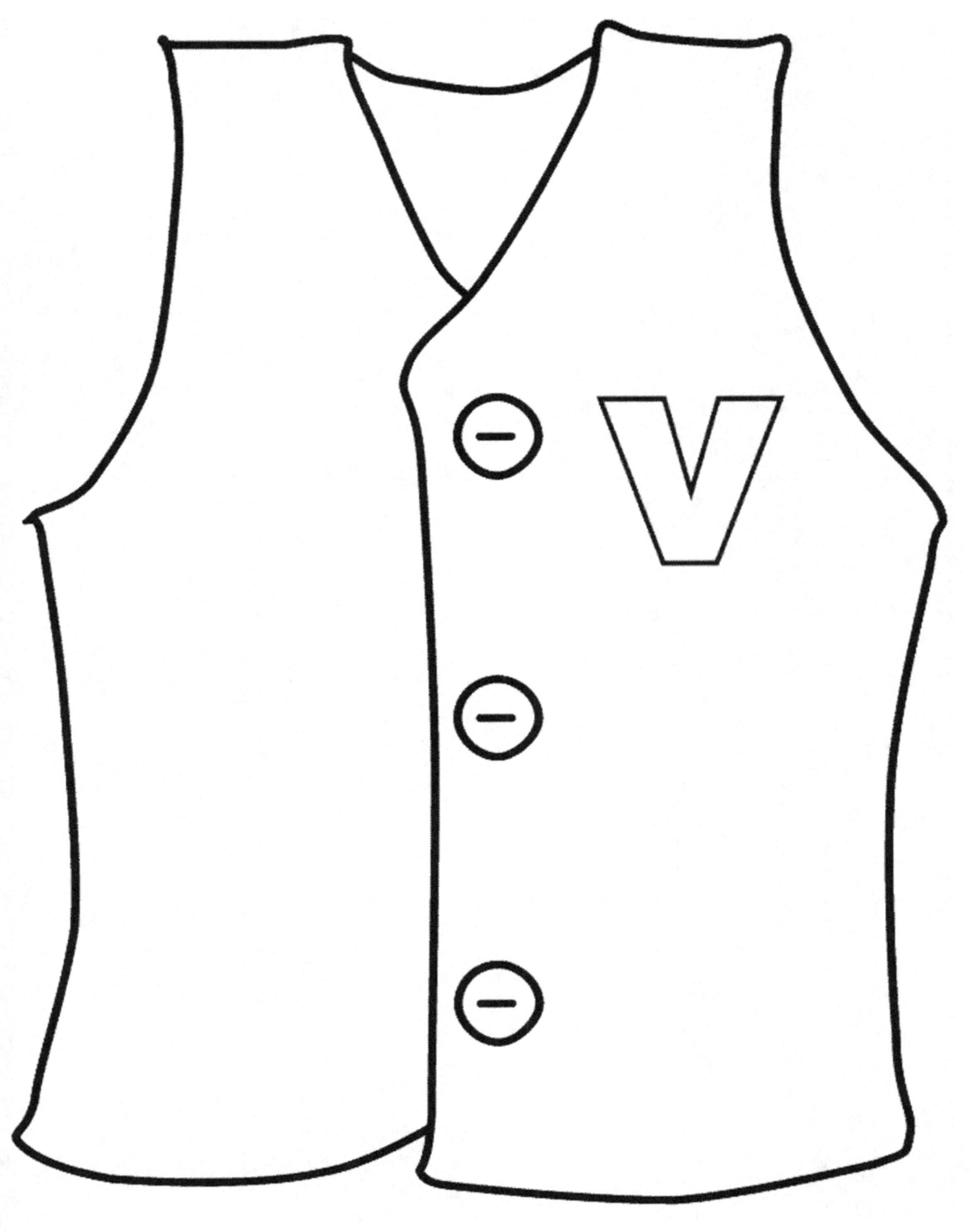

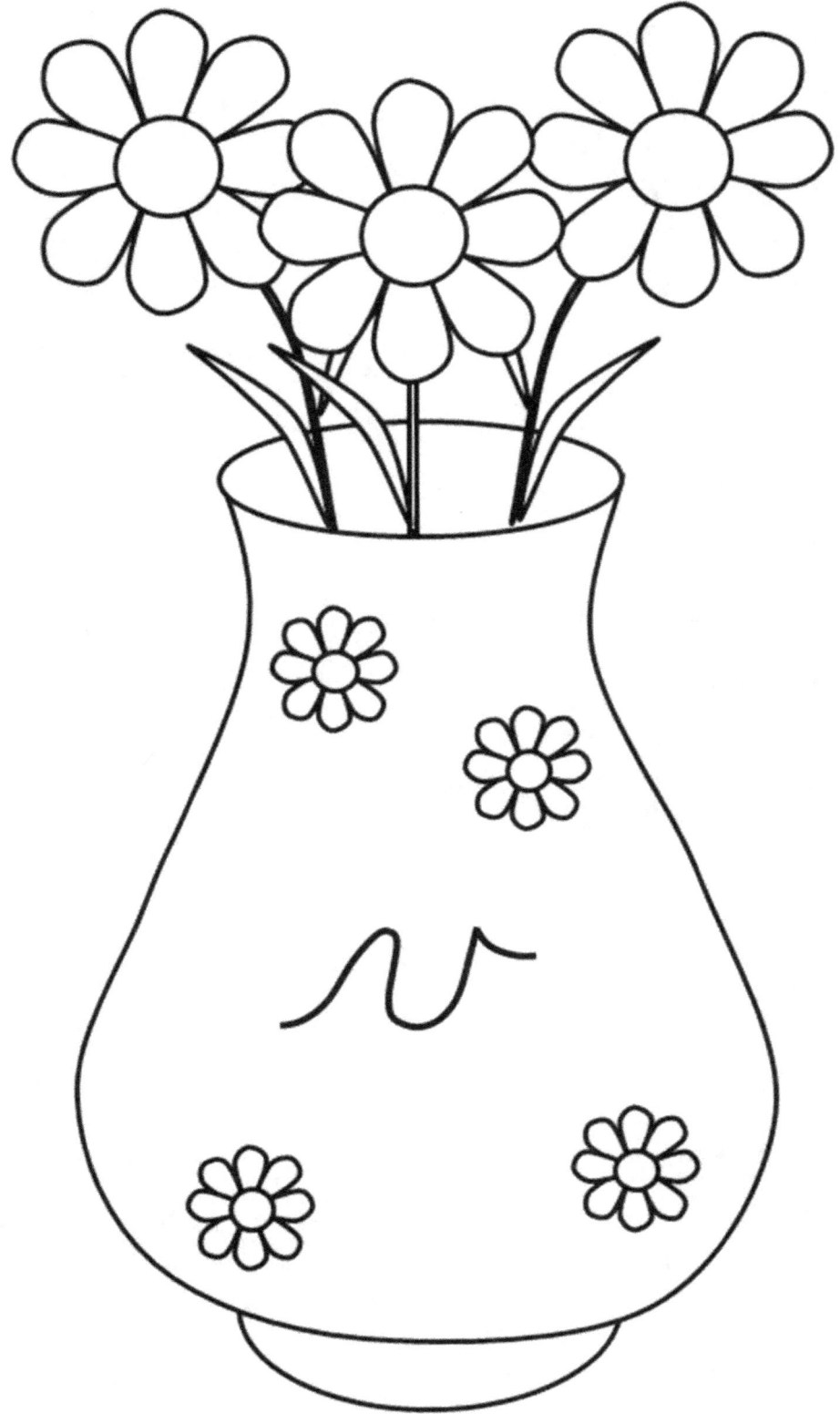

Trace the steps for making the letter v on the following line.

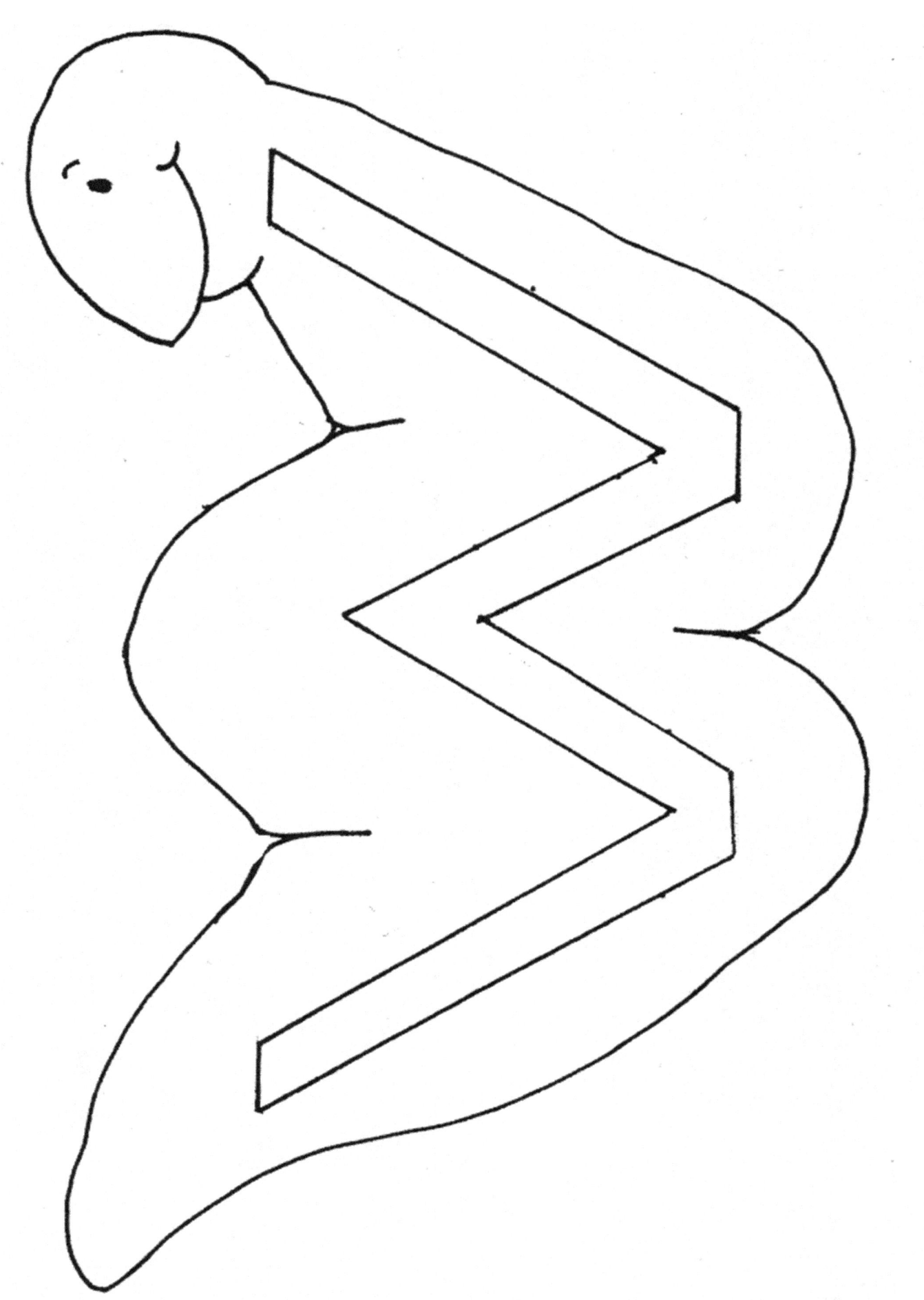

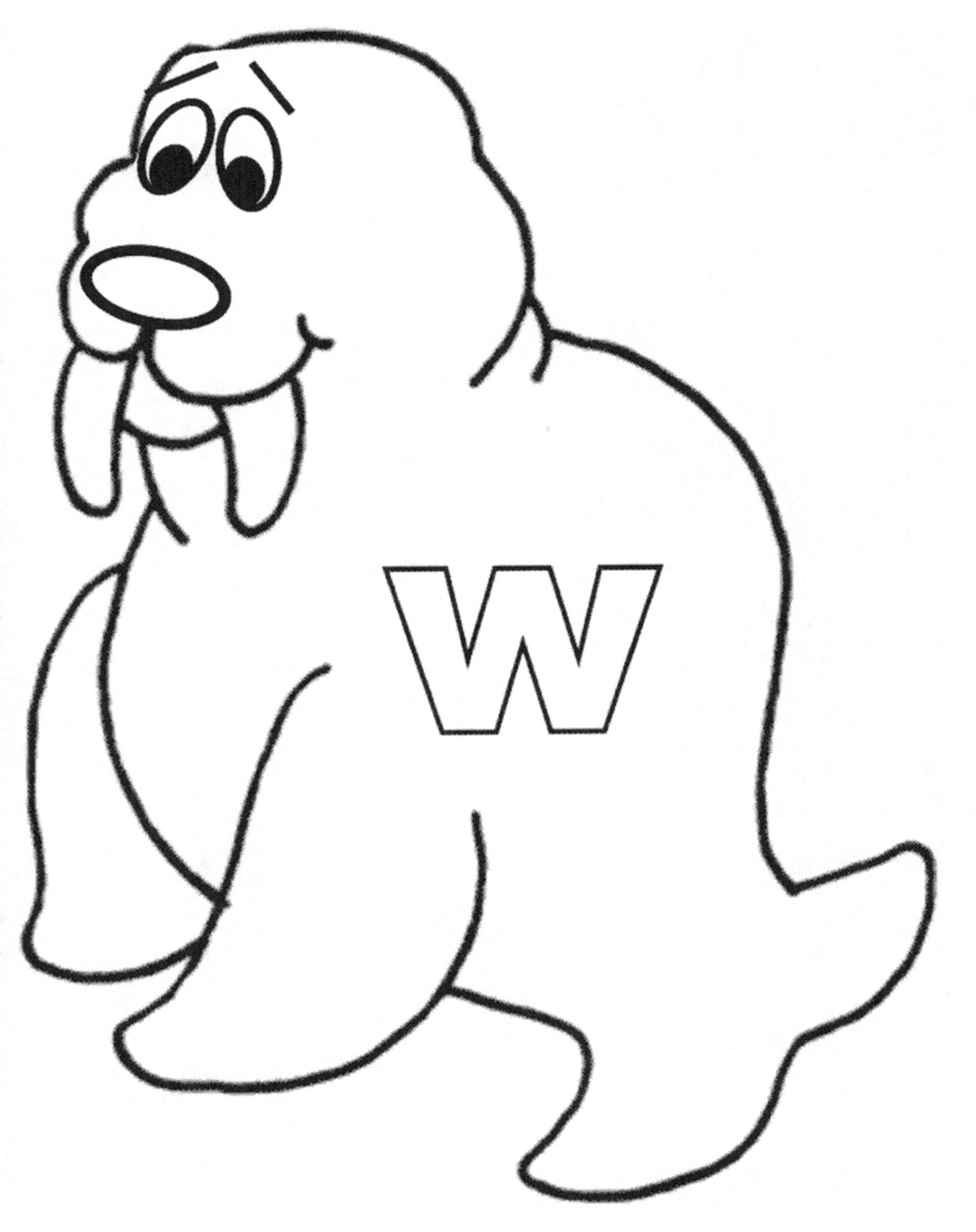

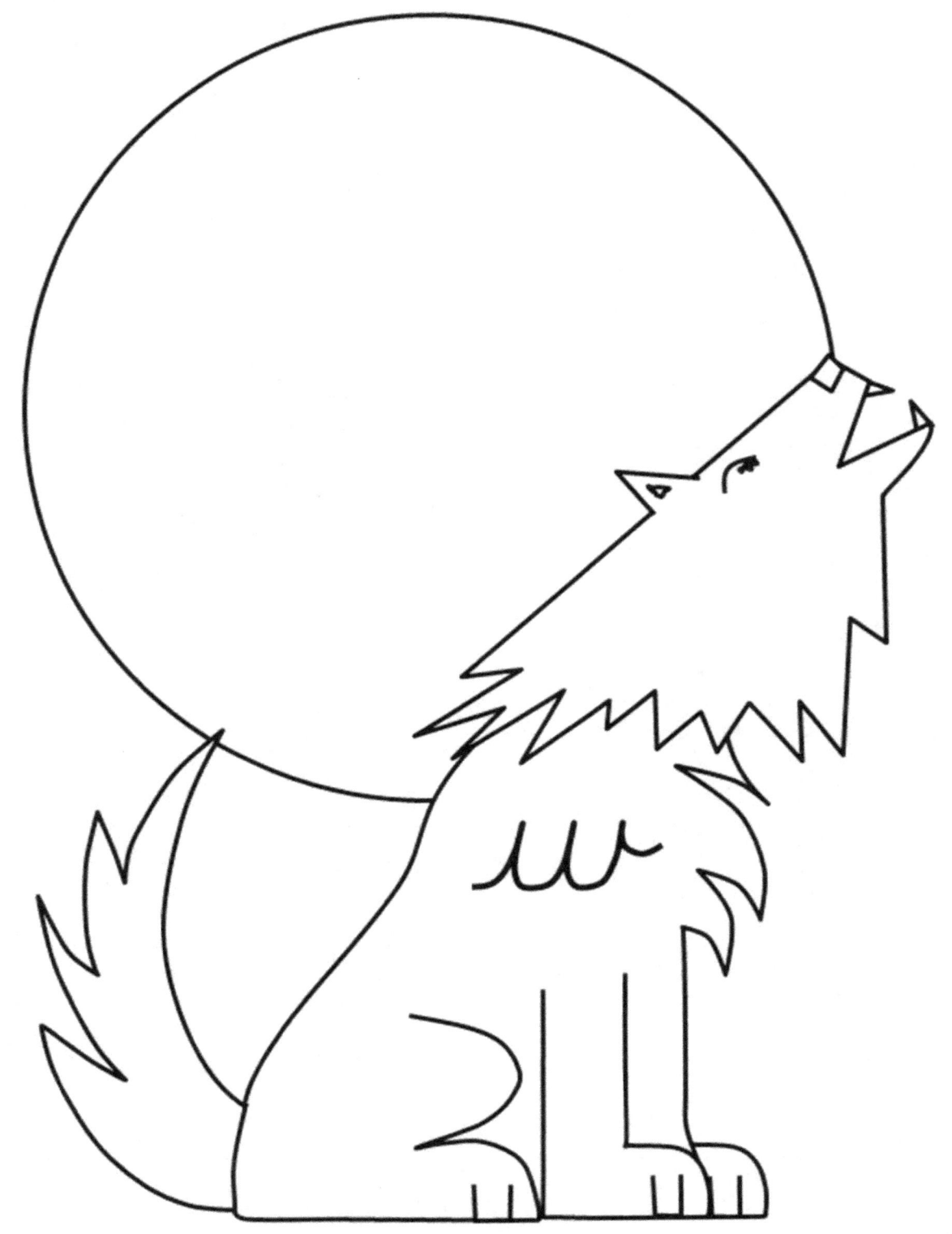

Trace the steps for making the letter w on the following line.

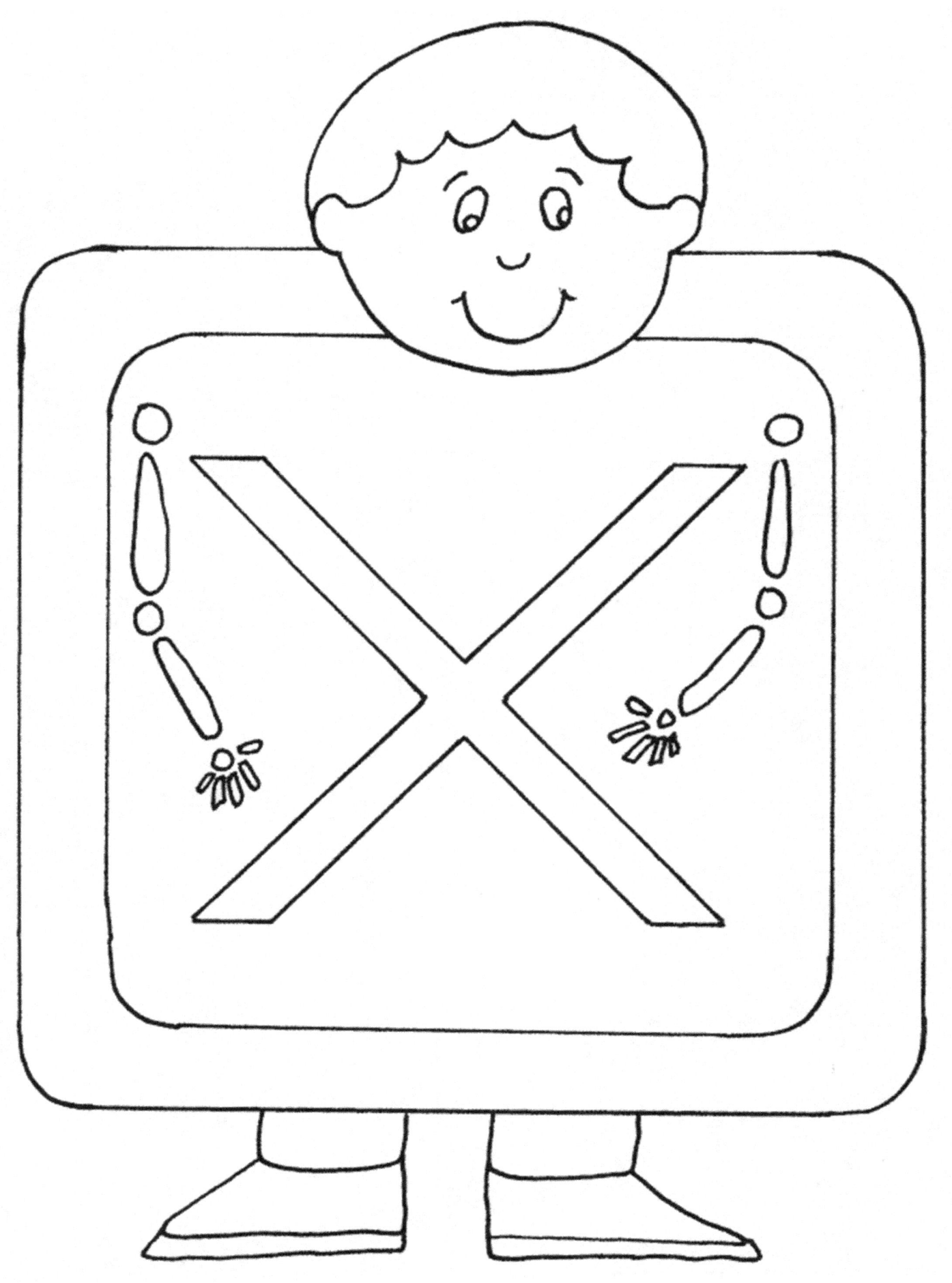

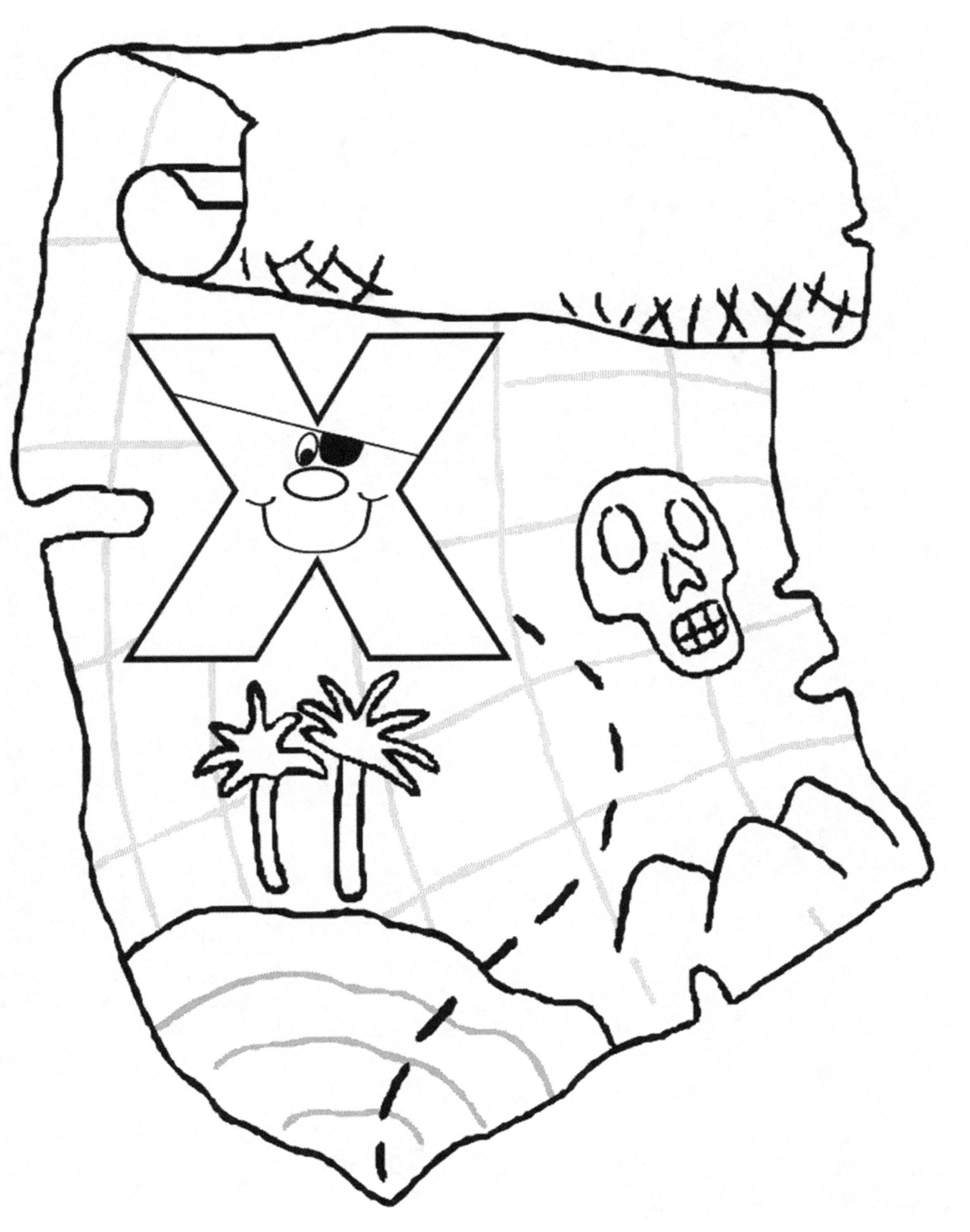

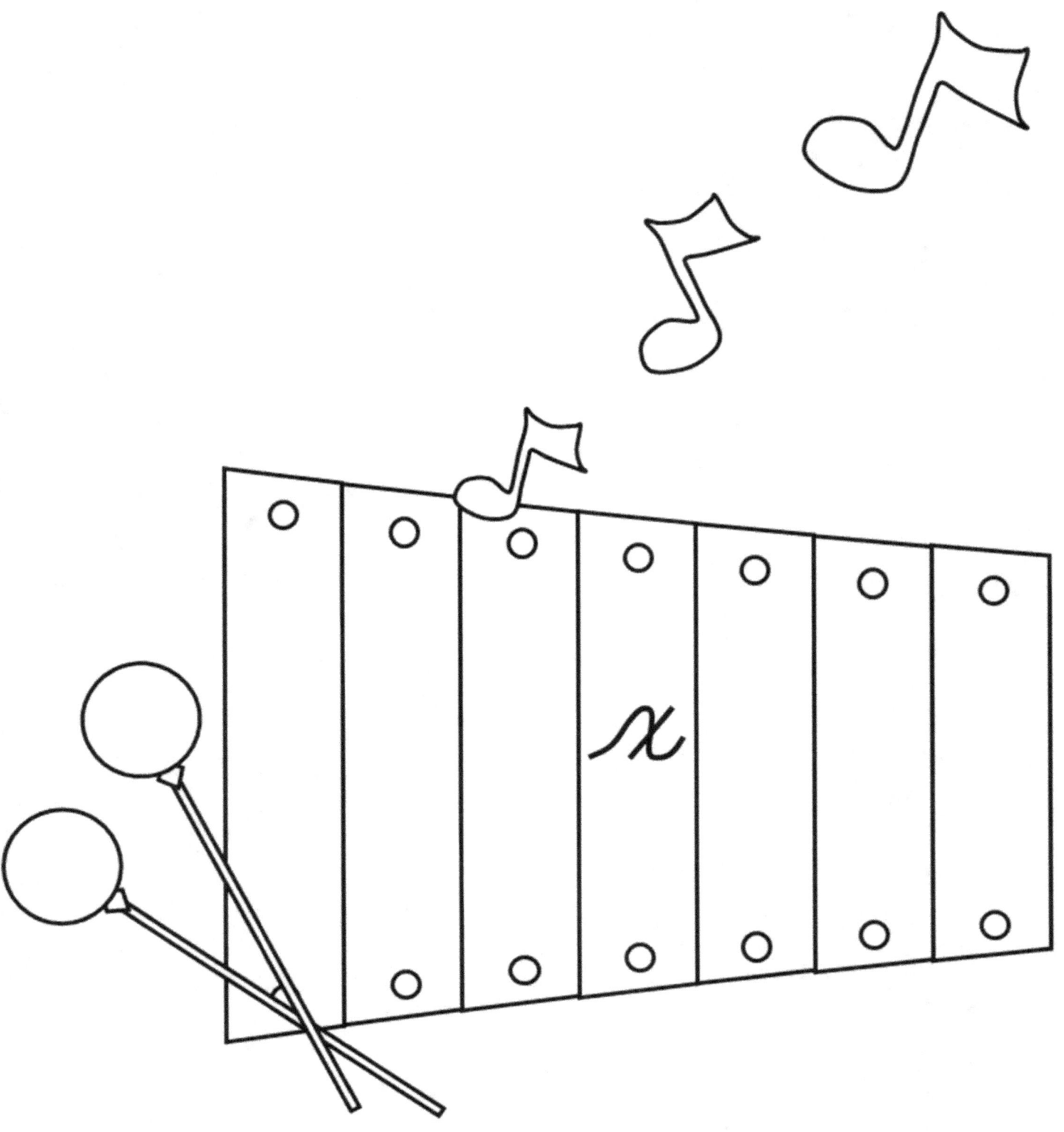

Trace the steps for making the letter x on the following line.

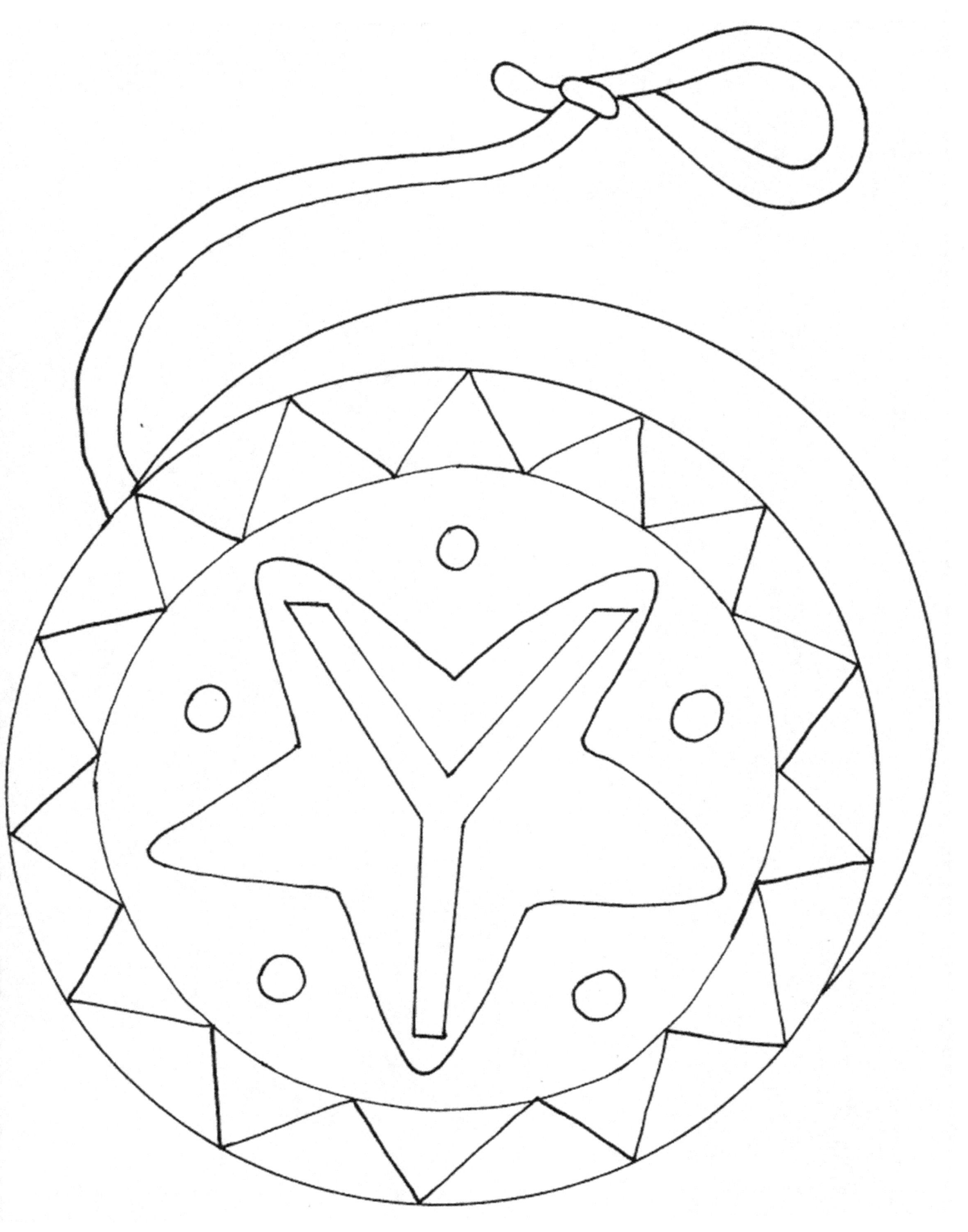

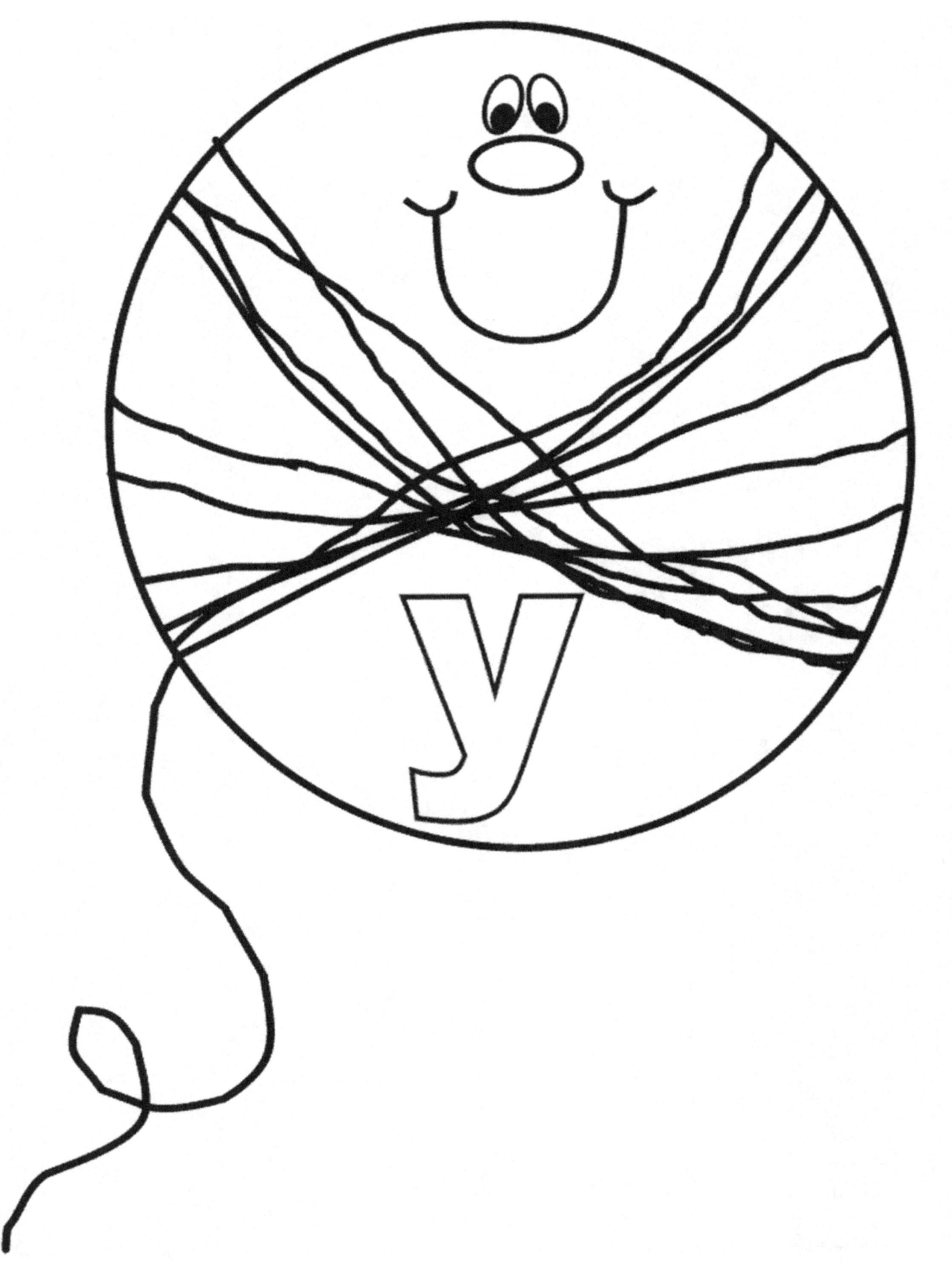

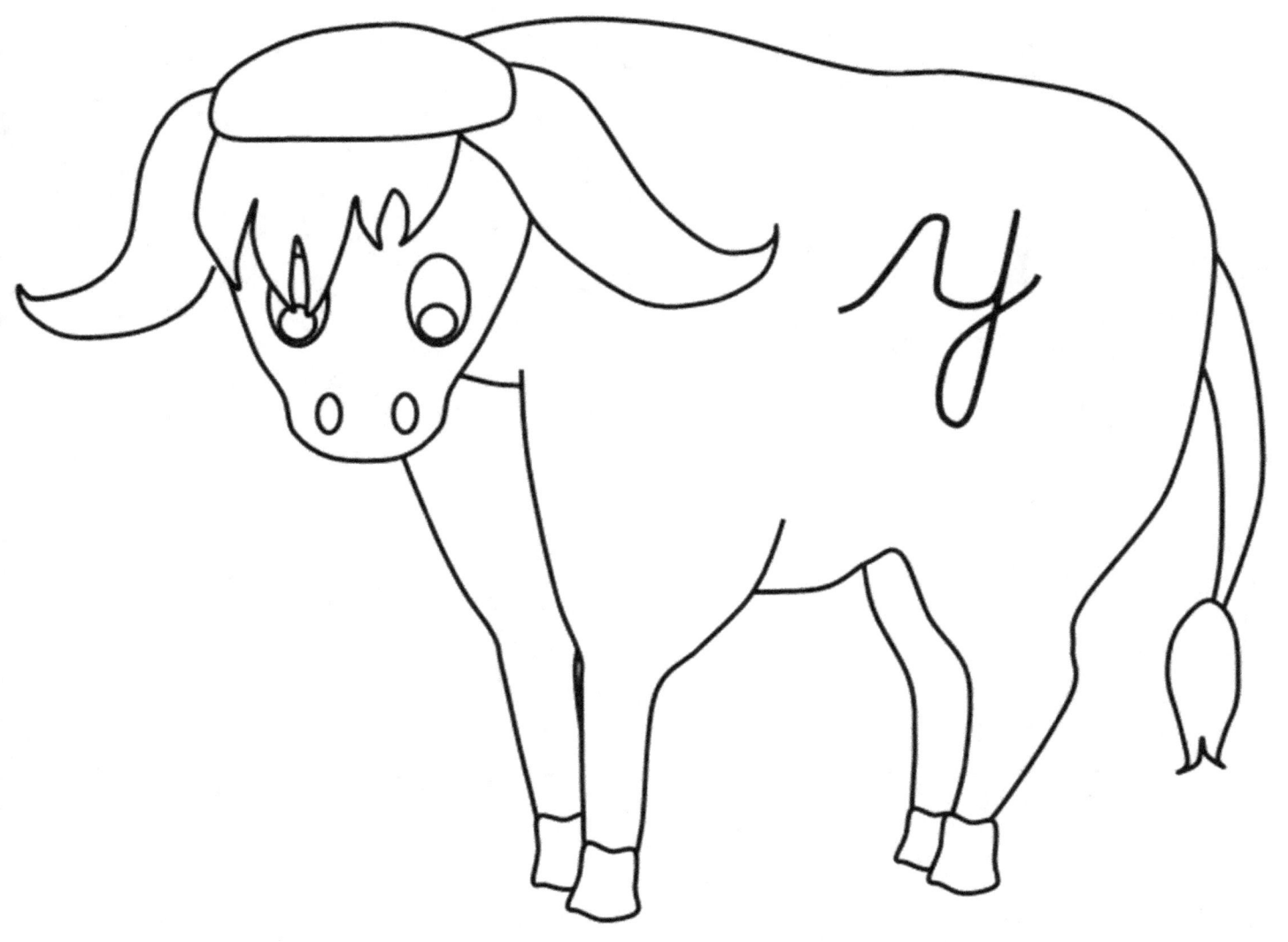

Trace the steps for making the letter y on the following line.

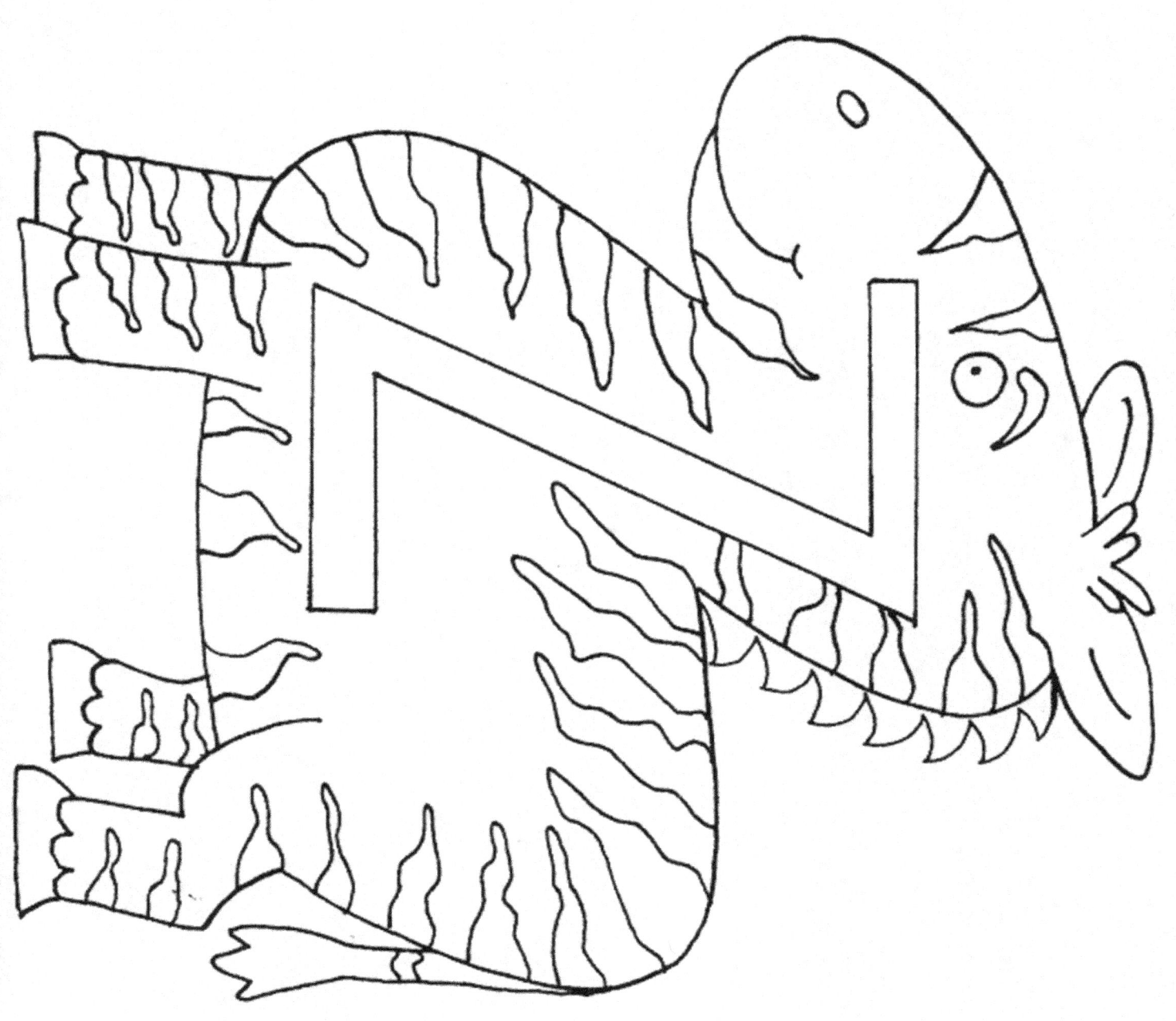

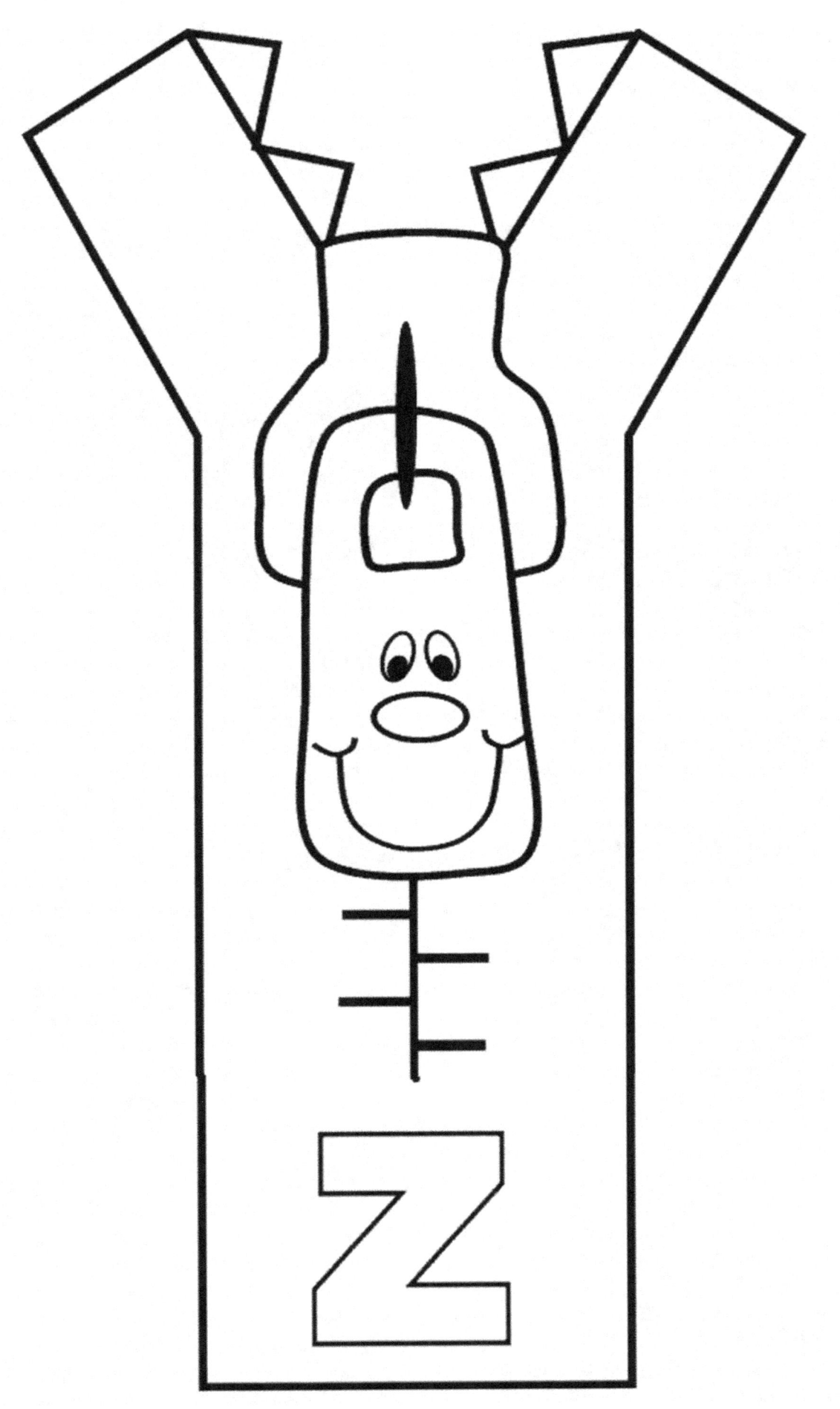

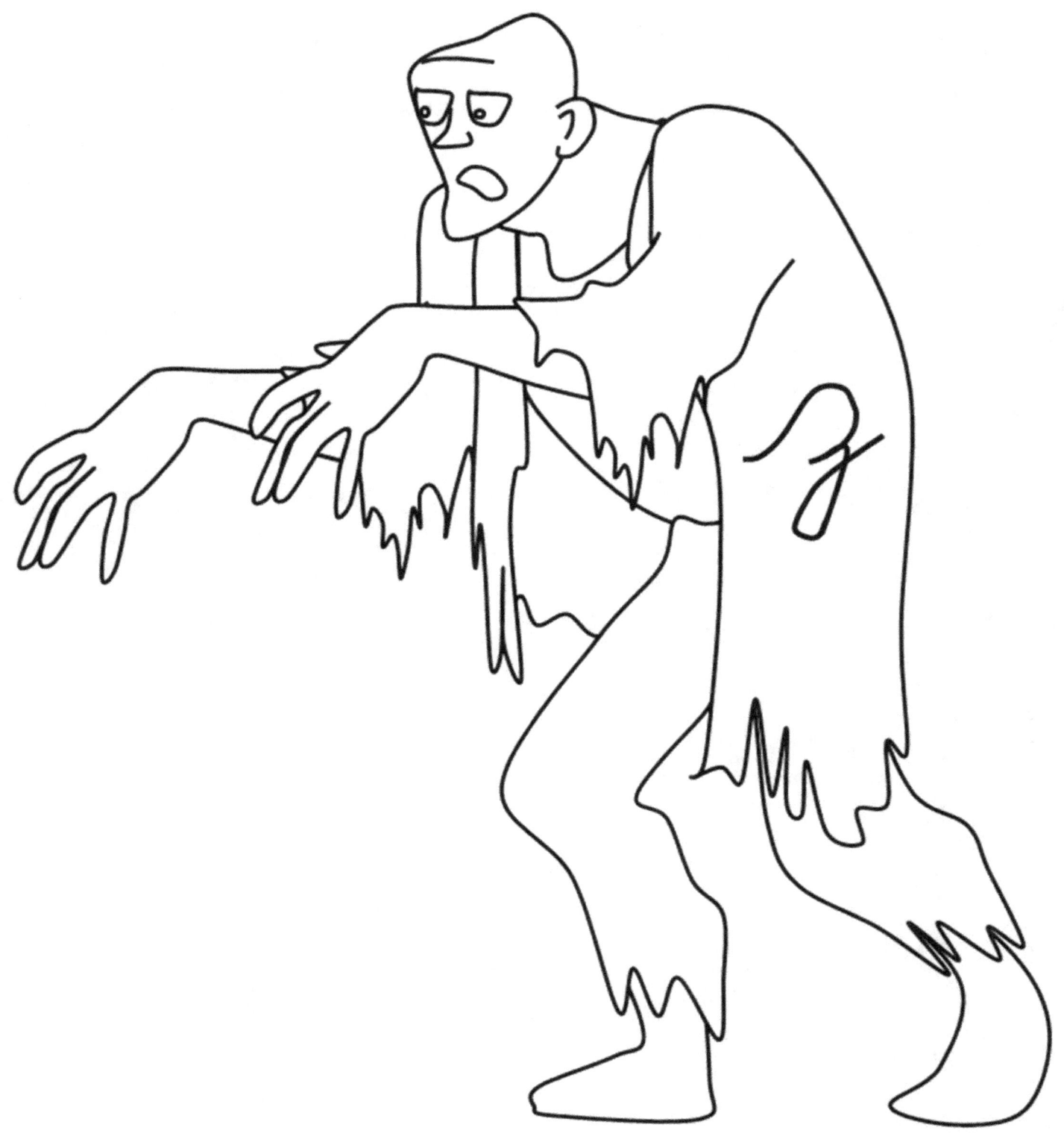

Trace the steps for making the letter z on the following line.

_z_ _z_ _z_ _z_ _z_ _z_ _zz_